PRO QUARTERBACK

My Own Story

---

by

JOHNNY UNITAS

and

Ed Fitzgerald

SIMON AND SCHUSTER
NEW YORK

FIRST PRINTING

LIBRARY OF CONGRESS CATALOG CARD NUMBER: 65–22266

MANUFACTURED IN THE UNITED STATES OF AMERICA
BY THE BOOK PRESS, BRATTLEBORO, VT.
DESIGNED BY EDITH FOWLER

FOR DOROTHY
and Liby

CHAPTER ONE

THE FIRST TIME I ever played in a training camp game with the Colts, I quarterbacked both teams, the white jerseys and the blue. I would run over to the side lines every time the ball changed hands, pull off one jersey and put on the other. No matter how it came out, I was sure to be on the winner, and I think I've enjoyed training camp ever since.

A letter comes from the head coach along about the first of May every year, saying how he feels about what we did last year and what he thinks we ought to be able to do this year, and that's when you know training camp is getting close. Especially if you play in the Pro Bowl game in January, the season stretches out pretty long, and it's always a shock to realize that it's almost time to get back to work. But it's a good feeling, too.

Don Shula's letter to me on May 1, 1964, had this to say:

DEAR JOHN:
In analyzing the 1963 season, our record of eight wins and six losses was very much indicative of the way we

played—a third-place football team. Any ballplayer that is satisfied with that record and third place should stay home and not report to training camp.

My biggest disappointment in 1963 was the inability to win the *big games* or the games that would have turned our season around—two losses to the Bears, two to the Packers, and the opening-day loss to the Giants. In these ball games a big play by either an offensive or defensive player at the right time could have made us the winner. Instead, we had the big letdown, and the other team made the play that won the game.

From our opening-day loss until the end of the season, we fought a continued uphill battle to get over the .500 mark. This cannot happen again; we must get off fast and be in contention, and when the big games come up we must win.

In order to make us better, I think each and every one should decide right now that 1964 has to be *our* year. Report to camp in the best shape ever. Be willing to sacrifice and pay any price that is necessary to make you the best, and in turn, *us* the best.

This training camp is going to be a tough, hard-hitting one with two objectives:

(1) to come up with our forty best players, and

(2) to get off to a flying start.

If you are not ready to go, both mentally and physically, when camp opens, it will only hinder your chances of being one of the '64 Colts.

This year, as last, I'm going to insist on a low reporting weight. Your weight will be 196. If you do not meet your reporting weight, your case will be discussed, and if you are not at the weight by Saturday A.M., July 25, the fine thereafter will be $10 per pound per day. Reporting overweight only indicates reporting "not ready."

We all feel that during the second half of the 1963 season we were the best team in pro football. We had winning momentum. Unfortunately, half a season is not enough. In 1964, we go all out for the World's Championship.

Sincerely,

DON SHULA

Head Coach

I might not feel so cheerful about camp if, like a lot of fellows, my wife and family lived somewhere on the other side of the country. But we train every year from about mid-July to mid-September at Western Maryland College in Westminster, Maryland, which is about forty miles from downtown Baltimore and only about thirty miles from where I live, in the little town of Lutherville. So even though we have to eat all of our meals in camp and I can't sneak home for dinner, I do get to see Dorothy and the kids every once in a while, at least once a week. and the time goes by fairly quickly. When we were getting ready for the 1964 season I had my oldest boy, Johnny—he's nine, Janice Ann is ten, Chris is seven and Bobby is four—out at the camp with me for two weeks in July. He slept in an extra bed they put up for him in the corner room on the third floor of the Gamma Beta Chi house that has been mine for the last eight years. He loved every minute of it. He used to get out on the practice field with a gang of kids before we came down from the clubhouse, and they would all place-kick and throw passes and break their necks trying to make fancy catches to show off to the people sitting in the stands and on the grass alongside the field. They tell me that little John looked like a good receiver but couldn't throw very much. He must have got a good workout for himself every day because he ate like a horse in the mess hall, which is set up for us in the college dining room and operated by the college personnel. The food is always good and there is plenty of it, as there would have to be for a crowd like ours. They always serve the main dish to us on a plate, and everything else, salad and vegetables and bread and butter, is heaped high on each table in big serving dishes, family style. We get steak a couple of times a week, roast beef, lamb chops and pork chops, veal cutlets, lunch hamburgers and fish—all good food. We get a lot of local corn, grown in the fields around Westminster, and it's delicious. The amount of that corn we put away is amazing.

The physical setup at Western Maryland is ideal for our purposes. We live in a few dormitories lining a pleasant quadrangle at the top of the hill above the practice field. Both the gym, where we dress, shower and hold our meetings, and the dining room, where we eat, are close by. The school practice field, which is the only one we use, is just a short run down the hill and is very inviting, with lots of big trees along the side lines. As you approach the field from the end zone below the school buildings, you see six tennis courts on one side and parts of a nine-hole golf course on the other two sides. Because the school is within easy driving distance of Baltimore on Route 140, there are usually a hundred or so people scattered around watching practice, and on weekend afternoons there is likely to be a crowd of four or five hundred, including a lot of the players' families and friends. Western Maryland has a summer school in session while we're there, so quite a few of the students turn out, too. You can generally manage to tell the players' wives from the college girls because they're a few years older and a whole lot prettier. There are hot dog, lemonade and ice cream stands, and some people bring picnic lunches. It's a pleasant country setting and it almost makes you forget your aches and pains and bruises. There is even a little private-plane airport, which is used as a base by a glider club, just across the highway, and whenever we have nothing else to do we can watch the gliders cut loose from their tow planes and play around in the wind with nothing but their big wooden wings to carry them from where they are to where they want to go.

I've always thought it is interesting to compare a pro football training camp with a baseball camp. Baseball teams, even in spring training, are always fenced off from the fans. It's hard for a kid, or a grownup for that matter, to get at one of the players. But there are never any fences around us when we're in training, and it's the easiest thing in the world to hit up a football player for an autograph or just talk to him for a minute. People are always taking pictures of us and having us sign autographs and in general acting as though we're all old friends. Little kids run up to us as we leave the field for the gym and either carry or wear our helmets up to the gym door. Sometimes they turn out to be children of our own ballplayers, but it doesn't make any difference whether they are or not. They're all welcome. I know baseball probably has a worse injury problem than we have—thrown or batted balls could cause a lot of damage if kids were allowed to run all over the place—but there ought to be some happy medium. I think we make a lot of loyal fans at training camp every year.

While we're in camp we get paid $6 a day, $42 in cash every Friday, above and beyond what is called for in our regular season's contract. We used to get $50 for each exhibition game, and nothing else, but that has been changed—for the better, I think. To a kid fresh out of college and trying to make the club, it means a lot. It's probably the only money he sees every week until—if he is lucky enough to stick—the season starts and he begins to collect a real pay check. We usually start out with about sixty players in camp and we are only allowed to keep forty on the roster, so there are a lot of disappointed kids (and some unhappy veterans) every August, when the cuts are made.

I think everybody who has been in this game for a while learns to dread the last big "cut" days, not just for himself but for the other guys, too. We were involved in some of the wheel-

11

ing and dealing, so I had a particular interest in the big fuss at the Giants' camp at Fairfield, Connecticut, on August 25, 1964. It was as good an example of the kind of unhappiness I'm talking about as the league has seen in a long time. Allie Sherman, the Giants' coach, dropped ten players in one day. Two of them, Hugh McElhenny, who saw his greatest days with the Forty-Niners, and Phil King, who had been the Giants' leading ground-gainer the year before, qualified as big-name players. So, in a different way, did Joe Don Looney, the club's number one draft pick and a young man whose reputation as a running back was almost as big as his reputation as a hard guy to handle. He had been suspended from the Oklahoma squad in his senior year "for the good of the team," which is unusual, to say the least. Another of the ten who got the ax was Glynn Griffing, the young Mississippi quarterback who had been number two behind Y. A. Tittle in 1963. Not as well known, but just as disappointed, were two holdovers from the year before, Louis Guy and Lou Kirouac, and four rookies, Millard Fleming, Bill Pashe, Frank Lasky, and Tom Costello.

King went to the Steelers for a high 1965 draft choice. McElhenny was released outright and later caught on with the Lions. Kirouac, an offensive tackle who sat out his rookie season with the Giants with a broken leg and who was highly recommended by our guard, Dan Sullivan, who had played with him and had been his roommate at Boston College, came to us along with Looney in exchange for two of our veterans, R. C. Owens and Andy Nelson. Owens, the old Forty-Niner who had been one of Y. A. Tittle's prime receivers when they were both at San Francisco, and Nelson, a solid defensive back who had been with us ever since we made our eleventh draft choice in 1957, were good football players for us, and it wasn't any easier for us to say goodbye to them than it was for the Giants to see fellows like King and McElhenny go—or, for that matter, than it had been for them to see Sam Huff go to the Redskins in a deal in the middle of April that must have been a real shocker to all of the Giants, including Sam. No matter how much practice you get, you never get used to the idea that the fellow whose locker is next to yours and who has been through so many hard football games with you and has bailed you out of so many tough spots is going to be on the other side of the line from now on. And every time you do your best to think of something comforting to say to a man who has just been traded, you are reminded that, one way or another, the same thing is going to happen to you one of these days. It may happen in the general manager's office, with the man telling you politely that he doesn't think you ought to try it any more, or it may happen more brutally, with the coach calling you into his office at the training camp and giving you a lot of malarkey about how they have made this deal for you because it's going to be good for you as well as for the club. No matter how they do it, it hurts.

It must have hurt Roy Walker real bad when we let him go at the end of August while we were getting ready for the '64 season. The year before, the newspapers had called Roy "the disappearing fullback" because he just went over the hill from camp one day and went back home to Cleveland. His father talked him into giving it another shot and he came back to us for a couple of days, but then he took off again, for keeps. Along about March or April of '64 he wrote a letter to Shula and asked for another chance, which Shula agreed to give him. He told us when he showed up in camp that he was ashamed of what he had done and that he wanted badly to make the club and was ready to work his tail off for it. He did, too. He never let up. But we just had too many fullbacks and he had to go. He left camp so fast that you knew he was hurting. He didn't even say goodbye to anybody.

But if it's tough on a young football player trying to make it, or just trying to prove something to himself, it has to be a

13

lot tougher on somebody like McElhenny. McElhenny was a big star in college, an All-American at Washington, and he had been a big star in our league for twelve years, mostly with the Forty-Niners and then with the Vikings and for one year with the Giants. They called him the King, and he could show just about a thousand yards gained on the ground for every year he had been in the league. But Allie Sherman sent the clubhouse boy to get him one early morning in August, and when the boy tapped him on the shoulder and gave him the message, McElhenny knew. When you're twenty-five and a big star, and the coach sends for you, it doesn't mean a thing. When you're thirty-five and the coach sends for you, you tighten up inside. And when he tells you you're through, it doesn't matter what words he uses or how much he tries to soften the blow. Your life can't ever be the same again.

The lucky ones are the ones who quit on their own, who never let themselves be talked into that one training camp too many. If I wish for anything out of football more than I've had, it's that I will know enough to quit that way. The time to leave the game is at the end of the season, not the beginning.

One way of beating the rap is to insist, if you can get away with it, on a contract that—depending on whether you're a rookie trying to make the club or a veteran trying to stay with it—calls for no cut or no trade. The clubs understandably don't like such clauses in their contracts, but, particularly in the cases of big-name college players who are in demand by both pro leagues, they are becoming more common. I've never had a no-trade clause in any of my contracts because I've always been more concerned with what I was paid than with who paid it to me, but it's easy to understand how a trade can be exceedingly painful to a player. Not only does it mean he has to uproot his family and try to put down new roots in a new town, but sometimes it means that he has to give up a good side-line job. Tommy McDonald lost a fine radio spot in

Philadelphia when the Eagles traded him to the Dallas Cowboys before the 1964 season. Sam Huff was assured by his boss, former Secretary of the Army Robert T. Stevens, that his selling job with J. P. Stevens & Co., the textile company, was safe whether he played for Washington or New York, but with another boss he might not have been so lucky. No wonder he said, "Pro football has got to be a two-way street. The player deserves some protection. The club can't expect him to give everything he's got year after year without giving him some assurance in return." Maybe Sam was huffy, but he had a right to be.

He didn't mellow very much after the season started, either. I read in the papers about his speaking at a Quarterback Club luncheon in New York soon after the Giants had beaten his new team, 13–10. "I didn't know it then but I know it now," Sam told a roomful of writers and fans. "For eight years here I was used as just a piece of equipment. I am only a piece of equipment with Washington. But I will play my heart out because that's the way this business is. It's a business. I'm in a business."

Who ever said it wasn't? But, as I keep saying, it's a business all the time except when you're out on the field with the ball. Then it's a game. Either that, or you don't belong in it.

It doesn't happen nearly so often as it does the other way around, but sometimes you find yourself saying hello in training camp to somebody you thought was gone from the club for good. It happened to us and to the Giants the same month of the big trade. We each got back a great thirty-eight-year-old player who had retired at the end of the 1963 season, Gino Marchetti for us and Andy Robustelli for them. Don Shula, and Carroll Rosenbloom too, for that matter, had been trying for months to persuade Gino to unretire himself. We all knew he was actually far from through when he quit to put in full time at his restaurant business—Gino has a string of hamburger stands all over the Baltimore area—and we knew we needed him back at defensive end to give us the kind of pass rush we would have to have if we were going to win. "Last year," Charley Winner, our defensive coach, said, "they were still putting two and three men on Gino to block him out. When they get down to one, we'll know he's had it." The Giants felt the same way about Robustelli, their fine defensive end. Andy had a good thing going for him in a successful sporting goods store, but they finally talked him into it. They probably used the same argument on him that Rosenbloom and Shula did on Gino—pride. The chances are that Robustelli also felt, as Gino did, that his club had been good to him and he owed them something. "Rosenbloom did a lot for me," Gino said. "He gave me a lot of help in business, and advice. If it weren't for him I'd still be working in a factory."

The plain truth is that just as the game itself is still as much of a game for us as it is a business, our relationships with the men who own the ball clubs often involve as much friendship as straight employer-to-employee dealing. It will be that way as long as most of the clubs are operated by men who care more about winning than they do about making a profit, men like Carroll Rosenbloom here in Baltimore, Art Rooney in Pittsburgh, the Mara brothers in New York, George Halas in Chicago, and George Marshall in Washington. They are all their own number one fans, and they get along with their players very well. It's hard not to like a guy who not only signs your pay checks but roots for you like a cheerleader and worries about you like a father.

It's probably the same psychology that makes you work as hard in practice as any college freshman or sophomore trying to make the team. You have to see one of our practices to believe how ferociously our ballplayers fight for a place on the squad. The linemen dig in with their heels and attack the sled with everything they've got, pushing against the weight of the machine and the coach riding it with all of their might. "Come on, give it a good pop!" you can hear the coach holler. Everything is a game, one line defending against the other's blocks, one secondary defending against the other's passes, one backfield trying to outdo the other on running plays. It's all done with a lot of slapping of hands on pants and noisy growling on takeoff, like a lot of lions or tigers let loose, and the total effect is enough to scare the daylights out of anybody who hasn't heard it all before.

No wonder I heard Bill Pellington, one of our oldest football players, sound a little beat when he answered a fan as he walked off the practice field in the summer of 1964 with one of his kids holding on to each hand and his pretty wife, Mickey, leading the parade. "How you feelin', Bill?" the fan wanted to know. Bill, his big head and his huge body dragging a little, said, "Pretty good for an old man. Legs are a little tired. We been goin' two a day, you know, and meetings every night. It's tough when you get to be my age." He wasn't kidding. You can imagine how Gino Marchetti felt along about the first of September.

Actually, Gino began to get back into it as early as our exhibition game with the Cardinals on August 21 in St. Louis. He played a little that night, by way of working in, and then he played almost three quarters the next week as we beat the Redskins in Washington, 41–14, before more than 45,000 people at D.C. Stadium. It was a good indication of the value of our exhibition or preseason games. I've heard people complain that we play those games only for money, that we don't really put out in them, but they don't know what they're talking about. The truth is that those games mean a lot to us. When you play only against your own personnel, you get to know them too well. It isn't a true test. To find out how much your rookies have to offer, and how much your veterans have lost, you've got to play the other league teams in preseason games. They're

17

real football games. We don't just go through the motions out there. We go at it full force. You don't have any choice, really, because if you take it easy and just fool around, some guy trying to win a job will take your head off.

What about getting hurt? Well, you can get hurt any time you go out on a football field. If you try to practice so you won't get hurt, then you will try to play so you won't get hurt, and you won't be any good either time. The way I see it, you have to take the chance, and the less you think about it, the less likely it is that anything will happen to you.

I've always been glad that we don't go in for hazing rookies at our camp. Some of the clubs in the league make a big thing of it, like the Lions, for instance, and the Giants. But we've never done it. I think it's humiliating to make a professional football player get up and sing his high school song or go through some kind of stupid initiation. The Colts aren't a fraternity; the only initiation that means anything to us is what happens in the football game. Every once in a while we have a camp show, but that includes both rookies and veterans, and it's strictly voluntary. The star of the last one was Jim Parker, who is a long way from a rookie but who is the funniest guy on the team in any kind of a situation. Jim can take off anybody —Rosenbloom, Kellett, Shula, me—and break up the audience every time. Jim is funny even when he is just being himself. To see him leaving the gym at Western Maryland after a practice, wearing a sports car driver's cap, dark sunglasses, a blue sport shirt, blue denim Bermuda-length shorts and leather sandals, smoking a pipe and driving a fire-engine-red convertible, is an experience. He had that outfit on once when his little boy came up to him as we were leaving the field at Western Maryland and asked if it was all right for him to ask Raymond Berry for his autograph. "Okay," Jim said, "let's see how you operate."

18

The little boy ran up to Raymond and held out his pad and a pen and said, "May I have your autograph, Mr. Berry?"

Raymond said, "Sure. What's your name, sonny?"

"My name is Jimmy Parker."

Raymond was busy writing his name, but he stopped short. "Jimmy Parker? You mean, you're Jim's son?"

"Yes, sir." Little Jimmy was as proud as a peacock.

"Well, now, would you say your father was a good football player?" Raymond asked him.

"Yes, sir," Jimmy said, very seriously. "He's the best."

"Aah," Raymond said, "you've been listening to him. That's what he tells everybody."

You can have fun in camp, and ease the pressure a little bit, without rubbing anybody's face in the dirt. I don't think there is any question at all that the hazing system cost the Giants a potentially valuable football player in Joe Don Looney. Looney started off with them with the handicap of his college reputation, which wasn't good, and when he rebelled at the hazing, they gave up on him right away. One of the things the Giants make their rookies do is help the trainer tape up all the veterans before practice every day. Looney wouldn't do it. He just flatly refused. I understand the club fined him a couple of hundred dollars for insubordination or something like that, and naturally, with a proud man like Looney, that didn't help any. So they ended up trading him to us.

The only trouble we had with him was when he got into an off-field scrape, ended up in court, and was fined and put on probation by a very angry judge. He was treated like everybody else when he joined us after the All-Star game, and we have high hopes for him. He's some football player, I want to tell you. As a quarterback, I've got to say that anybody who can't get along with a man like Looney, running and kicking

19

the way he can and liking combat the way he does, has got to have something wrong with him.

All Joe Don needed, really, was a little understanding and a lot of work. Shula gave him both, and it wasn't always easy.

There were times, I must admit, when it was downright difficult. Looney is a loner, a rugged individualist, and a little bit flaky. You never can tell what he is going to say or do. There was one time when we were on the road, and Ted Davis was rooming with him. Ted woke up out of a sound sleep at about one o'clock in the morning and saw Looney sitting in front of the television set with the blankets from his bed draped over both the set and his head. Ted was surprised, but the noise wasn't too bad and he didn't want to complain, so he just rolled over and went back to sleep. The next time he woke up, at about six A.M., Looney was gone. It must have been an hour later that Joe Don came walking in the door, the blankets wrapped around his head and shoulders Indian-style.

"Where you been?" Ted asked him.

"Out."

"Out where? Where could you go in the middle of the night?"

"I went over to the graveyard across the street and found me a nice gravestone to go to sleep on. I like graveyards. They're the most peaceful places there are."

Then there was the meeting that Shula called for ten o'clock in the morning, and Looney showed up at eleven. Shula bawled him out and told him it would cost him $25, and Looney just sort of shrugged his shoulders and turned around and started to walk out of the room. That really made Shula mad.

"Where are you going?" he wanted to know.

"I got a cheeseburger out in my locker," Looney said.

"Well, what would you like me to do," Shula asked him, and he was really burning, "hold up the meeting while you eat it?"

20

"No," Looney said, "I just thought I ought to go get somebody to watch it for me."

What are you going to do with a guy like that? We always kneel down together before every game—and after the game, too, win or lose—and say a quiet prayer. But not Looney. While the rest of us would be praying, Joe Don would go into the trainer's room, turn on some music on the radio, and do the mashed potato all by himself. But even that wasn't as completely Joe Don Looney as what he said when somebody asked him at our end-of-the-season party what he was going to do in the off-season. "Oh," he said cheerfully, "I've got a paper route lined up."

It's interesting to take a look at some of the things our players are taught in camp:

"In a ball game we tackle any way we can get ahold of them."

"Players are not permitted to associate with gamblers or persons of bad repute."

Those are two samples of the kind of information laid out for us in the football player's bible, the play book. Put together before summer practice by the coaching staff, and added to in loose-leaf style as the training camp and the regular season move along, the play book has a lot in it besides the actual diagrams of our two hundred or so plays. In addition to the warning to keep away from gamblers, there are such personal-conduct regulations as:

"No drinking in the camp dormitories."

"No hard liquor at any time."

"No firearms in camp."

"Camp bed check at eleven P.M., lights out at eleven-fifteen."

"All camp meals must be attended unless excused by head coach or trainer."

The book lists specific fines for most major offenses. The most popular number is $25, which it will cost you if you're

21

late for a meeting or a practice. Missing bed check is $100. Shula gives us a talk every year saying that if we know we are going to miss the check, we ought to be smart enough and grown-up enough to call in and say so, then drive back carefully. He would rather have us miss bed check and lose $100 and stay alive.

You can pay from $200 up for "acts detrimental to the team," which is a pretty broad category that can cover just about anything.

There is an executive committee of players appointed by the coach "to convey any thoughts the team might have for the betterment of the overall operation." The committee, which consists of three men from the defense, three from the offense and the three captains, offense, defense, and special teams, also has the power to hear appeals from players who have been assessed either "major or maximum" fines. Minor fines cannot be appealed.

Tackling is only one of the subjects that get special treatment in the book, but it's one of the most important. In addition to telling us to grab them, when the chips are down, any way we can get ahold of them, the book also says, "On a given day tackling attitude and efficiency is generally the first indication of the outcome of a ball game," and it puts the subject away for keeps with this blunt advice: "Gang tackling is the surest way to stop a ball carrier. Stop only when you hear the whistle!"

Blocking gets a full share of attention. "We do not use any brush or finesse blocking. We want the opponent *hit*. Have pride in your blocking. Strive to be the best blocker on the team. Ending up a block with your knees on the ground will be acceptable only if you are on all fours and keeping after your man."

The plays, of course, fill up most of the book. They are all there, under their particular designations—for example, Special

Plays, Draws, Aggressive, Split Block, Strong Side Flare, Weak Side Flare, All Out. Each of them has a special note addressed to the quarterback, like these:

"This pass is good vs. all coverages. A blitz should not hurt us."

"Check off vs. all defenses except 4–3 as this is a special pass for the 4–3 combination and man-for-man coverages."

"You must give clearance for pulling guard, yet as you reverse spin, do not force the ball carrier deep, or it will be difficult to get into the hole. Make a good bootleg fake. Watch for bootleg pass possibility."

"Do not type yourself as to time of use of draw plays, either as to down or position on the field."

I'm especially fond of this one, on one of our pass plays. "You will be protected against all blitzes except an all-out blitz." Well, hell, a quarterback can't expect everything.

CHAPTER TWO

Every once in a while, when I have to make a special effort to get to Mass before a ball game, or when we're at camp and I drive in a mile or so to Westminster and go to the seven o'clock Mass before breakfast, somebody asks me, "Why do you go to church so much?" I usually say something like, "Well, it can't do any harm," and let it go at that. But the truth is that I think God has been very good to me and my family and I like to say thank you every chance I get. I never bother, in church, with anything specific like praying that we win a football game. I just try to say thank you.

Of course, I was raised in Catholic schools, and they do a pretty good job of pounding it into you that you ought to go. I went through both grade school and high school at St. Justin's in Pittsburgh, my home town. My father's name was Leonard Unitas. He was a Lithuanian, and he owned a truck and used it to run a coal delivery service. He was a big, strong man, built a lot, I guess, like I am, about six feet one inch and a hundred and ninety-five pounds, my mother says. He caught pneumonia and died when my oldest brother, Len, was only ten, and my mother was left with Len, my sister Millicent, me, and my other sister, Shirley. She managed to keep the coal business going, taking the orders herself and hiring men to drive the truck for her until Len was old enough to do it. She also got a job nights doing cleaning work in downtown Pittsburgh office buildings. Later on, when the coal business got to be too much for her, she went to work in a bakery and sold insurance on the side. Then she studied bookkeeping in night school, passed a Civil Service exam for bookkeeper, and has been working for the city of Pittsburgh ever since. She married again, and her name is Mrs. Howard Gibbs now.

I've never quite understood exactly how Mom was able to keep the five of us fed and clothed in those early years, but she did it. We didn't have too much of anything, but we had enough. Len and I used to make a dollar here and a dollar there doing odd jobs. I used to specialize in shoveling coal that had been dumped in somebody's back yard into the bin in the cellar. I would get seventy-five cents a ton, and sometimes, on a Saturday, I might pick up three tons' worth of work and make two dollars and a quarter. When I got to be old enough, fifteen and sixteen, I used to work summers on construction gangs. None of that stuff did me any harm so far as building up my body was concerned. In fact I have no doubt I was lucky that I got to do it. I've been able to do my share of the work ever since.

I almost didn't grow up at all. When I was five years old, I ran down the street with my sister Shirley one evening when we saw my father's truck coming, and he stopped and let us climb up in the cab to ride the rest of the way to the house with him. Shirley was sitting in the middle and I was on the outside, next to the door. I guess I hadn't closed the door very well, because as soon as the truck started, I fell right out of the door and under the truck. I would have been a mess if Dad hadn't put on the brakes real quick. As it was, the right rear wheel was only a couple of inches from my head when he lifted me out from under.

Then, twice, I got into trouble with bullets. The first time, Len found an old cartridge in the woods and wedged it into a tree so we could throw rocks at it and try to make it explode. It exploded, all right, and I was standing right in front of it and got most of the stuff in my leg. They took me to the hospital in one of the neighbors' cars, and the doctor took out as much of the lead as he could find. He couldn't get all of it, though, and I always claim that's why I can't run any faster than I do. I was only about seven then, so there was some excuse for my being so stupid. There wasn't any the next time, which was when I was a junior in high school. There had been some robberies around the neighborhood, and Mom got hold of a .38 revolver to keep in the house, just in case. After we had had it for a while I decided I ought to clean it. I took the clip out and was holding the gun in my right hand while I reached out with my left for the cleaning rod and a patch, and then, don't ask me why, I pulled the trigger. Naturally, there was a bullet in the chamber, and it went right through the index finger on my right hand. So off I went to the hospital again, and I was lucky they were able to save my finger. I've never been able to bend the first joint of that finger since, but it hasn't bothered me any. Who knows, maybe it has helped. At first they said I wouldn't be able to play any football that year, but it turned out that if I wore a splint, consisting of a tongue depresser wrapped up in gauze and adhesive tape, I could throw the ball all right. In the end, I missed only one game.

I had been put at quarterback for the St. Justin's team when I was a sophomore. Freshmen weren't allowed to play on the varsity, so it was my first season. The coach had been playing me all over the place, but mostly at halfback and end, right up until a week before our first game, with St. Vincent's, when our quarterback broke his ankle. The coach had a bunch of us practice throwing the ball, and he decided I could do it well enough, so he made me the quarterback. I had less than a week to learn the whole offense, but I managed to get by, and I threw the ball pretty well in the game. So I was the quarterback from then on, even the next season, when we got a new coach, Max Carey.

In my senior year I made quarterback on the Pittsburgh All-Catholic High School team and even got an honorable mention on some magazine's All-America High School team. I wanted very much to go to college, mainly for the education and what it would mean to me later on, but because I wanted to play football, too. I remember when I was a little kid in grammar school and the sister asked us all in class one day to tell what we wanted to be when we grew up, I said I wanted to be a professional football player. I still had the idea in the back of my mind, and I knew that my only chance of taking the first step, going to college, was if I could get a football scholarship. My biggest hope was that Mr. Carey, who knew a lot of people, would be able to help me. He certainly tried. So did Father Thomas J. McCarthy, one of the priests at St. Justin's, who had particularly good connections at Notre Dame. Like a lot of Catholic boys who are crazy about football, I couldn't imagine anything more wonderful than going to Notre Dame. I was pretty excited when Father McCarthy fixed up a tryout for me there in April 1951, the spring of my senior year. He sent them some of the newspaper clippings about me, like the one in which Max Carey told the reporter, "This boy is one of the best passers and T-quarterbacks in Catholic League history. He threw twenty-two touchdown passes in 1949 and 1950, and he's also a very good runner and a fine defensive man." And the one that quoted Wilbert Rall, the coach of St. Wendelin's, as saying, "Unitas has been a real workhorse for his team and his coach. He was the backbone

27

of the St. Justin's ball club with his field generalship, his passing, kicking, running and defensive play. He's a very quiet and unassuming boy, but he's a package of dynamite on a football field. He's by far one of the finest passers in scholastic football."

That all made me sound too good to pass up, but even before I got out there the Notre Dame coaches told Father McCarthy they thought I was too light for them. I was tall, almost six feet, but I only weighed a hundred and thirty-eight pounds, and they didn't think I would be able to last in the kind of league they played in. But I went out there with a lot of hope just the same. I had Father McCarthy behind me, and Fritz Wilson, a Miller High Life distributor in Pittsburgh who was friendly with Fred Miller, the head of the beer company and one of the most influential Notre Dame alumni in the country. All I wanted was a chance to show what I could do.

The colleges don't like to call visits like the one I made to Notre Dame tryouts, but that's what they are. I was disappointed to find out, when I got off the train at South Bend, that Frank Leahy, the head coach, was out of town and wouldn't be able to see me, but Bernie Crimmins, the old All-America who was Leahy's backfield coach, kept me around for a whole week and gave me a real good look. In the end, he sent me back home without saying anything. Then, a week or so later, he called up Coach Carey and told him he was sorry but they had decided not to offer me a scholarship. They were interested in me, Crimmins said, but they didn't think I was big enough. Carey tried to talk him out of it, arguing that I might be light now but I had a big body with good bones and I was sure to put on a lot of solid weight in the next couple of years. But Crimmins said they didn't think they ought to take the chance, and there went Notre Dame for me.

I don't remember who set it up, probably Coach Carey, but my next expedition was to Indiana. I flew out there with Richie

28

McCabe of North Catholic High, and we worked out together for a couple of the coaches. But we weren't even invited to stay overnight. They just shook hands with us after the workout and thanked us for coming and told us we could go back home, and that was the last we ever heard from them. Not even a telephone call or a letter saying they were sorry but they couldn't use us. Nothing.

The natural place for me to think about next was Pittsburgh. John Chickerneo, who played quarterback on Jock Sutherland's last great Pitt team, the one with the "Dream Backfield" of Chickerneo, Harold Stebbins, Dick Cassiano and Marshall Goldberg, was a freshman coach at the university then, and he had seen me play a couple of times and had talked to me about coming to Pitt. When I came back from Notre Dame he showed so much interest in me that I began to take it for granted that I would go there. Then Chickerneo got a job coaching a high school team in Pittsburgh, and I guess he was the only one at the university who knew or cared anything about me, because when he left, the interest just died—and I was right back where I had been when Notre Dame turned me down, nowhere.

The worst part of it all was that I was wasting an awful lot of valuable time. Then, out of the blue, Len Casanova, the head coach at Pittsburgh, asked both Richie McCabe and me to work out for him. We were glad to do it, and Casanova looked us over carefully for four days. When he thought he had seen enough, he offered us both scholarships to Pitt. I was relieved, and so happy about it, I could hardly believe it. I might have known there would be a catch somewhere, and there was—only this time the catch was all my own doing. I failed the entrance examination.

I had been going steady for quite a while then with the girl I married, Dorothy Jean Hoelle. We had begun to date while I was a junior at St. Justin's and she was a sophomore.

We got together on a bus taking the basketball team and some students to a game in Johnstown. Dorothy and a couple of her girl friends were standing in the aisle and I got up and gave her my seat. When we were getting off the bus I asked her to save me a seat for the ride back, and she did. Then I walked her home. It was snowing, I remember, and we talked a lot and liked each other and I asked her for a date and she said yes. So from then on we went out together all the time, although sometimes, when it was to a dance, it was a kind of strange arrangement because I would take her to the dance and see her in and then sit outside in the car while she danced with all of the boys, because I didn't like to dance. But anyway, Dorothy knew me about as well as anybody, and she couldn't believe it when I failed the exam at Pittsburgh. Neither could I. I wasn't anything special as a student, but I wasn't that bad, either. Those nuns didn't let you be that bad at St. Justin's. But there it was. I had failed, and nobody was saying anything about giving me a second chance.

I was saved by something that happened when Max Carey went to a coaches' clinic run by Paul Brown of the Cleveland Browns. While he was there he struck up a friendship with John Dromo, one of the assistant coaches at the University of Louisville. When Dromo mentioned that Louisville had the makings of a pretty good football team if they could only get their hands on a good passer, Carey told him about me, and Dromo was interested. Carey explained to him that I probably was going to Pittsburgh, but he told him a lot about me, anyway, and Dromo must have talked it all over with the Louisville head coach, Frank Camp, because Mr. Camp invited me to come down to Louisville for a tryout. I went, and worked out, and the coach offered me a scholarship.

It was nice to know that somebody wanted me, but I wasn't sure I would be doing myself much good going to such a small school. Like everybody who follows pro football, I knew that there was no law against a player from a small college making the National Football League. (Look at Alex Sandusky, who comes from Clarion State Teachers, where they play teams like Slippery Rock Normal and St. Mary's Girls School.) But I also knew that your chances, especially if you are a quarterback, are a whole lot better if you have played for a school that gets some attention in the newspapers. So I kept hoping that something else would turn up. But nothing did, and Camp and Dromo kept after me. Their argument was that I would be better off being a big fish in a small pond like Louisville than a very small fish in a Big Ten pond. Dromo had coached George Ratterman in high school and he told me all about how unhappy Ratterman had been at Notre Dame, where he didn't do much for four years except caddy for Johnny Lujack, filling in now and then when the big man was out. I finally got the message and decided it wasn't a bad deal for me.

At Coach Camp's suggestion I went down to Louisville early in July and took the entrance exam so I could enroll in the summer school. The coach thought it would be useful for me to pick up a few extra credits and just sort of get started on the studies so it would be easier for me in the fall. He also wanted to have me around for a little football practice on the side. But I still wasn't in shape to win any Rhodes scholarships and I didn't pass the exam. I stayed in Louisville, though, working for the Brown and Williamson tobacco company, doing cleanup work in the factory after hours, putting away a little money for the clothes and things I would need during the school year. I went home for a week in August, then went back to Louisville to appear before the college entrance board.

They asked me to tell them just why I wanted to go to the college and why I thought they ought to give me a chance even though I had failed the summer school entrance exam. I talked to them as honestly as I knew how and made it plain that I wanted very much to earn a college degree and thought I could do it. They agreed to admit me for the first semester on probation, which meant that I could carry only a carefully limited number of courses until I had proved that I could handle the work load. My scholarship came from the athletic department and covered my room, board, books and tuition, with a monthly payment of $25 to cover incidentals, laundry and that kind of thing. Except for the summers, I didn't hold down a job while I went to Louisville. I don't think I could have done it and played football and passed my classwork, too.

I liked the college a lot. The coach was a good man and if he knew you were working for him he would do anything for you. Actually, he almost sent me home twice that fall because he was afraid that I was so thin I would get hurt. I lived on the campus in a dormitory that had been built by the Navy during the war for V-12 officer candidates. Each football player had a room of his own, and it was very comfortable. As far as the football team was concerned, I was on the varsity squad even though I was only a freshman, but I was the third of three quarterbacks and it didn't look as though I would play more than a few minutes at a time, every now and then, just for the experience.

That all changed, though, when we lost three of our first four games, to Boston University, Cincinnati and Xavier. The coach liked the way I threw the ball, and I guess he figured that if he was going to lose anyway he might as well lose with me and make sure I would be ready to do him some good next year. He started me in a game against St. Bonaventure at Olean, New York, on the same field where, four years later, I had such a bad time trying to win a job with the Steelers. It rained all afternoon but the Bonnies' quarterback, Ted Marchibroda, and I kept throwing the ball anyway. They had us down, 19-0, at the half, but in the second half I completed eleven straight passes, three of them for touchdowns, and we went ahead, 21-19. Even when they kicked a field goal near the end to beat us by one point, 22–21, I felt pretty good about the way everything had gone. I felt even better when the coach told the Louisville papers that he was going to go with me as his quarterback for the rest of the season.

The good game against St. Bonaventure did wonders for everybody's morale. I know that when you lose, you lose, and they don't put footnotes in the record book to explain how well you played while you were losing, but every once in a while there is such a thing as a moral victory—and that's what our game with the Bonnies was, if there ever was one. We bounced back to beat North Carolina State, Houston, Washington and Lee, and Mississippi Southern, and that made our record for the season a respectable five and four. I threw eight touchdown passes in the four games we won, but more important, I learned something about being a quarterback. I learned that the first thing is that you have to take charge. It's hard, especially for a freshman, to start telling the other guys what to do, and to be hard-nosed about it if somebody wants to know who appointed you our leader, but you're not going to be any kind of a quarterback unless you do it.

The biggest win we had that first year of mine at Louisville was over Houston. They had 19 points on us in the odds, but we beat them, 35–28. It didn't look so good for us in the beginning. Houston scored on their second offensive play after a bad kick of ours had given them the ball on our twenty-seven. They made the extra point, too, and had us down 7–0 before the game had hardly started. But after one of our halfbacks, Bill Karns, picked off a Houston pass and took it back to their twenty-three, we got the touchdown on three plays, two on the ground and one on a pass I threw to Karns. We made the point and it was all tied up, 7–7. We moved the ball pretty well after that. We went 85 yards for our next touchdown, doing it mostly with passes, and at the end of the half we were ahead, 14–7. I had completed eight out of nine.

33

We made it 21–7 early in the second half, mostly because Houston fumbled and we recovered the ball on their thirty. We got it over in four plays, all of them on the ground. But after that we had our troubles for a while. They gave our defense fits and had us tied, 21–21, early in the fourth quarter. They were stopping us in the line, too, and there wasn't much I could do except throw. We got up to the Houston forty and came to a fourth-down-and-two situation.

It was getting late in the game and I couldn't see giving up the ball, but neither could I see us getting those two yards hitting the line. Not the way those guys had been belting us around. So I didn't take it very well when one of our junior backs, Bill Pence, said, as soon as we got into the huddle, "Give me the ball. I'll get the two yards."

It must have sounded funny because I was just a skinny kid, but I really let him have it. "When I want you to take it," I told him, "I'll let you know." And I called a pass.

When we came out of the huddle I could see that Houston was counting on a run. They were lined up tight, shoulder to shoulder, no daylight at all between them. I took the ball from the center, dropped back, looked for our best end, Dave Rivenbark, and threw him the ball in the middle of the open field. He was all by himself, and all he had to do was keep from falling down the rest of the way.

Bill Pence was good-natured about it. He came up to me and said something like, okay, he wouldn't argue with me any more, but that wasn't what was important. What was important was that I had learned that you can't run a football game by having the committee meet and take a vote. Somebody has got to be the man who says what to do, and it had better be the quarterback.

Maybe I was a little too enterprising on the play that got us our last touchdown, but I've never thought so, even though I know I almost threw Coach Camp into shock. Houston had quick-kicked us and the ball had rolled dead on our four-yard line. I sent two plays into the line, and we picked up three yards. Then, on third down, I decided the last thing in the world they would be looking for was a pass, so I went back to the end zone and hit Babe Ray on the forty. Everybody including the safety man had been playing in tight, so Ray had no trouble running the ball down the field, and we had our insurance touchdown. I know I would have looked pretty foolish if it hadn't worked, but I'm a firm believer in the theory that you can't surprise anybody unless you take a chance.

Unhappily, that was the last winning season we had while I was at Louisville. We lost fifteen of our scholarship football players at the beginning of my sophomore year, and that ruined us. The university had just got a new president, and he set up a minimum standing that everybody out for any sport had to maintain. It wasn't that it was unfairly strict, but the trouble was that there were a lot of our guys who were pretty far below the mark when the new man came in. They might have caught up if he had been willing to wait a little while and give them a chance. But he wouldn't. So they kicked out fifteen football players and a bunch of assorted basketball players, baseball players and whatnot. Maybe they were just trying to economize on scholarships.

Anyway, we didn't have much of a football team left. We had only nineteen men out for spring practice and we filled out the squad in the fall with freshmen. It was a rough year. When you're playing schools like Dayton, Chattanooga, and Cincinnati with kids just out of high school, you don't have too much of a chance. Our best game was a 41–14 win over Florida State at Tallahassee, which I remember well because one time when they were coming at me from all directions I got desperate and threw a shovel pass between my legs and a guy actually caught it for a fifteen-yard gain. Mostly, though, we got ourselves killed every Saturday.

The way things were going, and the way they looked as though they would be going the rest of the time I would be there, I was tempted pretty hard when I got a chance to transfer away from Louisville. Bernie Crimmins, the man who had turned me down at Notre Dame, had become the head coach at Indiana, and he had been keeping an eye on me. He was short of quarterbacks and he thought I could help him. He came all the way down to Louisville to see me in the spring of my sophomore year and he talked to me like a Dutch uncle. I would be a lot better off playing in the Big Ten, anyway, he said, but with our ball club torn to pieces the way it had been by the school, there was simply no point in my staying at Louisville. He said the first thing we would do was to get a ruling from the commissioner of the Western Conference, which is the official name of the Big Ten, on how much eligibility I would have left if I transferred. He knew I would have to sit out a year without playing ball but he didn't think that year would count against my eligibility. He thought I would lose only the two years I had played at Louisville and would still have two years left to play. Which, he thought, would make the transfer worthwhile. It would give me a real chance to show what I could do and to build a national reputation that might make all the difference when I tried to get into professional football.

I told Crimmins I would think it over. Before I did anything, I said, I would want to talk to Coach Camp and Coach Dromo and to the Louisville newspapermen who had been so good to me. I would want to talk to some of the football players, too. I didn't want to do anything underhanded. Crimmins said fine, that was a good idea, and he went back to Indiana.

The guys on the team said I was crazy not to do it, that I would never get any important recognition playing for Louisville, especially the way things were now, and that if I was serious about wanting to play professionally I had to start

36

with the fact that Indiana would do me a lot more good than Louisville would. But I called home a couple of times and talked to my mother and my brother, and to Dorothy, and none of them thought it was such a hot idea to leave a school where I was being treated so well.

After I talked to my old high school coach Max Carey, I pretty well made up my mind not to do it. "It's a decision you'll have to make for yourself," Carey told me, "but I will say this much. When you needed this guy Crimmins, he didn't want you. Now that he wants you, he thinks you ought to come running. Are you sure you want to sit around for a year doing nothing? What if the Army grabs you then? You may never finish college."

I've never been sorry that I called Crimmins and told him I appreciated his interest in me but that I was going to stay where I was and make the best of it. The more I thought about it the more it seemed to me that it would be a pretty ungrateful thing to walk out on Coach Camp after he had offered me a scholarship when nobody else would and then had stood up for me to help get me into the school after I had failed the entrance exam.

I won't deny that I felt a little jealous on Sunday morning every now and then, reading about Indiana's big games with schools like Minnesota and Illinois and Northwestern and Purdue, particularly when I had spent all Saturday afternoon on my back in a losing game, which was most of the time. We won only three games in my sophomore season and not very many in my junior and senior seasons. I remember Tennessee played us, I guess as a sort of a breather, in 1953 at Knoxville, and beat us 59–6. I think they must have scored four touchdowns in the first five minutes. I was playing safety and one of the reporters told me after the game that I had made 85 percent of the tackles for our side. If I made that many tackles playing safety, you can imagine how easy it was for those guys to tear up our line. After the first quarter they sent their first team into the dressing room and they never did come back out. They played their second and third teams for the rest of the game.

My senior year would have been bad enough anyway, but it was made even worse by an accident in practice. We were scrimmaging, the week before our opening game against Murray, when I made a bad throw and the pass was intercepted. I followed the ball downfield and was just getting ready to make the tackle when somebody hit me from behind. In the tangle, I cracked my ankle—a hairline fracture, they called it. At first they thought it was just a bad sprain, but the swelling didn't go down at all, so they took X rays and found out about the fracture.

Except for the first game, I played every game on the schedule with the ankle taped up, but I didn't have too much mobility. Sometimes it was all I could do to get back fast enough to take a look around and throw the ball. And not being able to run, and having everybody know it, didn't help me any. I've always been able to run pretty well when it was necessary, and that makes the defense a little more careful about coming in on me. But I wasn't fooling anybody that year. I was strictly out there to throw the ball, and they knew it, and they sent everybody but the waterboy in after me as soon as the ball was snapped.

The coach asked me, before I had played in a game, if I wanted to sit out the whole year and let my ankle heal and then play as a senior in 1955. But by then I knew I was going to marry Dorothy Hoelle if she would have me, which I thought she would, and I didn't have any intention of staying in college any longer than I had to.

Actually, Dorothy and I didn't even wait for me to graduate before we got married. We celebrated the end of the football season by having my Uncle Constantine, my mother's brother, who is Father Constantine Superfisky (and from whom I get my middle name), marry us on November 20, 1954, in the same church where he had baptized me as an infant—the Church of the Resurrection in Brookline, Pennsylvania. We got married on Thanksgiving vacation so we could have a few days to take a trip somewhere, but the way things worked out we didn't get very far because Dorothy got homesick. But that's another story and I think I will let her tell it. It wasn't long, anyway, before I was not only back in school but even out of it, diploma and all, ready to go to work for a living.

There never was any doubt in my mind that I wanted to play in the National Football League. My hopes shot up during the summer when the league held its annual draft meeting and the Pittsburgh Steelers made me their ninth pick. Being picked ninth didn't mean that I was sure of getting a place on the club, but I thought it at least meant that I was sure of getting a chance to show what I could do. I felt pretty good putting in a hard day's work on a construction gang while I waited for the time to come to report to the Steelers' camp on the St. Bonaventure campus. I had been glad to sign the contract they had sent me, for $5,500 for the season. I knew that the contract didn't mean a thing unless I made the team. If they cut me before the season started, I would be out of luck. But I thought I was ready to take my shot.

The trouble was, nobody ever let me shoot. Maybe I wasn't going to Mass often enough in those days. Anyway, I found myself out in the cold without an overcoat. Walt Kiesling, the coach, didn't pay as much attention to me as he did to the assistant clubhouse boy. I might just as well not have been there. To tell the truth, I'm not convinced Kiesling would have known I was there if the Associated Press hadn't put out a picture of me showing a Chinese nun how to hold a football. The picture got into the papers all over the country, so if Kiesling read the papers, he probably knew I was in camp. But you can't prove it by me. Kiesling had Jim Finks as his number one quarterback, and right from the start of the camp season he used Vic Eaton of Missouri as number two, even though they had drafted Eaton two rounds after me.

I've often wondered if Kiesling and his staff cooled on me before they ever saw me because they found out about my troubles with the entrance exams at Pitt and Louisville and decided that I was too dumb to make a big-league quarterback. Nobody ever told me that, but it makes sense out of a situation that doesn't make much sense any other way you look at it.

I stayed with the Steelers through five preseason exhibition games, and they never played me for a minute. The only action I ever saw was in a couple of scrimmages. I threw two touchdown passes and got away for a twenty-five-yard run in the scrimmages, but I guess nobody was looking. I knew for sure my number was up when Ted Marchibroda, who had been number two behind Finks before he was drafted, was discharged from the service and came back to the ball club. They put Marchibroda in the first exhibition game we played after he came back even though he had been in camp only a couple of days. I still sat on the bench. I think the longest talk I ever had with coach Kiesling was when he called me into his office and told me that he had too many quarterbacks now and couldn't use me.

The worst thing they had done to me was to keep me hanging around so long when they obviously had no intention of giving me a job. With the season just about ready to start, it meant that I had no time to try to catch on with somebody else. I was sore, and I let Kiesling know about it. He couldn't give me any reason at all for giving up on me except that he had more quarterbacks than he could use, and I told him I thought it was his fault that I hadn't had a chance to show him whether I was better than the others or not. I don't like to be a pop-off, but I didn't hold back that time.

The only encouragement Kiesling gave me was to tell me that the club would be playing their home opener in a few weeks against Philadelphia, and if I would come to see him at the ball park he would talk to me about a job on the band team—what they call the taxi squad now. That meant that if the owner, Art Rooney, approved, I would be put on the payroll at whatever figure they felt like paying me, maybe $50 a week, maybe $100 a week (more likely $50), and would show up for practice every day and learn the system and be ready to come up to the club roster if all of their quarterbacks suddenly got hurt at the same time.

Incidentally, when I say he paid me off, that doesn't mean there was any big money involved. NFL contract salaries don't become effective until the regular season starts. The club had been giving us $12 a week for spending money, so I got the last of that plus bus fare back home to Pittsburgh. It added up to so few dollars altogether that I didn't feel I ought to spend any of it on a bus ticket. I hitchhiked home.

It was about as bad a day as I've ever known, much worse than when they told me no at Notre Dame and even worse than the day I failed the exam at Pitt. I was a married man now, in fact a brand-new father. Dorothy and I had a tiny baby girl we had named Janice Ann, and if Dorothy's parents hadn't invited us all to stay in their house, I would never have been able to quit the construction job long enough to try out for the Steelers. Now it was all for nothing. I would have been a lot better off working for those couple of months. I would have been at least a thousand dollars ahead. With things like that on my mind, no wonder Dorothy said, when I walked in the house, "John, whatever's the matter? You look like half past six."

Actually, she knew what had happened. She had read it in the afternoon newspaper. Another nice touch about the Steelers was that Dorothy had been in the club offices that morning to pick up some tickets for the game with the Eagles, and nobody had mentioned the fact that I had been cut. But I guess, as they say, nobody likes to talk about rope in the presence of the condemned man.

Dorothy was learning the hard way what it's like to be married to a professional athlete. She did everything she could do to cheer me up and to keep me from feeling discouraged. The main thing was that she made it plain that if I wasn't ready to give up, neither was she. And I wasn't.

The first thing I did the next morning was to send a telegram to Paul Brown, the coach of the champion Cleveland Browns, asking for a chance to try out for his club. I had some reason for hoping that Mr. Brown might be interested in me. One of Coach Camp's good friends was Dick Gallagher, who scouted for the Browns, and Camp had always kept Gallagher informed of what I was doing. The coach and I had had lunch with him one day before I graduated, and he had said that if I was still around in the late rounds of the draft his club would probably pick me up and invite me to camp. That had gone out the window when the Steelers, who weren't interested in me at all, had drafted me the ninth time around.

But I did know that they knew I was alive, and I also knew that they had looked bad at quarterback in the All-Star game that summer. Otto Graham had retired after the Browns walloped the Lions, 56–10, in the championship game at the end of the 1954 season, and neither Babe Parilli nor George Ratterman had looked very good as the All-Stars beat the Browns, 30–27, for one of their few wins over the pros. I had a hunch Mr. Brown was a little unhappy, and I was hoping he would be willing to take a look at me.

At least he took the trouble to call me up and talk it over with me, for which I was grateful. But what he had to tell me was that because he was dissatisfied with his quarterbacks, he had talked Graham into unretiring, and he thought he was all set for this season with either Ratterman or Parilli as Otto's

42

backup. He told me that if I wanted to come to their camp next year and try out for the club, he would be glad to have me. I thanked him and told him that if I was still looking for a job then, he would surely hear from me.

I went to the Steelers–Eagles game on Sunday and watched the Eagles win it, 24–22. After the game I went down to the locker room and hung around outside the door for a few minutes, figuring I would give Kiesling a chance to settle down. When I saw Nick Skorich, the line coach, come out, I went up to him and told him that I would like to talk to Kiesling about the taxi squad job. But Nick didn't think I ought to do it right now. "He's pretty mad," he said. "Why don't you wait until tomorrow and come out to the Schenley and talk to him there?"

I didn't want to be a nuisance, so I said, sure, that was all right with me. The next day I took a bus out to the Hotel Schenley and saw Kiesling with Mr. Rooney. I got Kiesling aside and asked him if he had asked Mr. Rooney about me yet, and he said no, he hadn't.

"We're going on the road again for a couple of weeks," he said. "Why don't you call me when we get back to town?"

I said I would, and I did. But when I got him on the phone he said that the club wouldn't go along with the idea of hiring me, and that was that. He never even suggested that I ought to come back to camp next season. When I hung up that time I knew that not only were the Steelers through with me, I was through with them.

My old construction gang was still willing to take me on, so I went back to work with them, this time as a pile driver, and an old college friend of mine from Louisville, Freddie Zangaro, got me a job playing quarterback for a semipro team, the Bloomfield Rams. The Rams were in the Greater Pittsburgh League, and they played every Thursday night at the Arsenal Street School in the Bloomfield section of the city.

It wasn't very fancy football. There was no grass on the field

43

and all of the players had to get out and sprinkle it with oil before every game to keep the dust down. The biggest crowd we ever got was a couple of hundred people, and we didn't get that many very often. No matter how many people came, I was paid $6 a game. The manager, Chuck Rogers, gave us our money right after the game in the club meeting room in the basement of Parise's Dairy on Liberty Avenue. I was glad to have the chance to play, and glad to take home the $6 to Dorothy. I know all of the newspaper and magazine writers have made a gag out of the $6 a game ever since I made it with the Colts, but I don't think any of them have ever understood that what mattered the most to us was not the $6 but the fact that there was a football team that wanted me. I was making about $125 a week on my job, and we were still living with the Hoelles, so we weren't starving to death. But what I needed was the chance to prove that I could play football. The $6 that I gave to Dorothy every week was important not because I had earned it but because I had earned it playing football. The wonderful thing about Dorothy, who was expecting our second baby, was that she understood the difference.

The hardest thing for me was the way the guys I played with and against needled me about the National League. They all knew, of course, that I had been in camp with the Steelers and had been cut. They kept asking me if I was going to go back to camp again next summer, and, trying to be honest, I would say yes, but I wasn't sure if it would be with the Steelers or with the Browns. They thought that was pretty funny, and although I didn't agree with them, I guess I can now. It must have seemed comical for a $6-a-game quarterback on the sandlots to be talking about playing with the Pittsburgh Steelers or the Cleveland Browns. The Browns had a pretty good quarterback named Otto Graham. Who needed Johnny Unitas?

What happened to me when Don Kellett, the general manager

of the Colts, called me one day in February 1956 just goes to prove that lightning can strike anywhere. I was out on the job when Dorothy picked up the telephone and was told that Mr. Kellett of the Colts wanted to talk to me. The girl who spoke to her explained carefully who Mr. Kellett was, and Dorothy said she wished she could get hold of me but there wasn't any way she could. I would be home at about six o'clock, she said, and would Mr. Kellett please call back then? The girl said yes, Mr. Kellett would.

He did. We had just finished our supper when the telephone rang. As a matter of fact, I had just started arguing with Dorothy about whether I ought to hang around the house and wait for the call. I wanted to go out bowling with a couple of guys from the job. She was sure Kellett would call back and she thought I ought to wait. I guess I just didn't want to sit around and be disappointed if nothing happened. But, anyway, there he was on the phone, and he wanted me to come to Baltimore in April, he said, to work out for Weeb Ewbank, their coach. If Ewbank liked me, they would give a contract and I would report to their training camp at Western Maryland in July. The contract, he said matter-of-factly, would be for $7,000. I said yes to everything, and that's how, for the price of a telephone call between Baltimore and Pittsburgh, I became the property of the Colts.

People are always asking me what the real story is of how the Colts happened to stumble on me, and there always have been two separate stories printed about it. One is that Kellett ran across my name while he was looking over an old league waiver list and remembered that I had been drafted pretty high up by Pittsburgh and, with his club badly in need of a quarterback, thought it couldn't do any harm to take a look at me. The other is that some fan of the Bloomfield Rams wrote a letter to the Colts' office saying that the Rams had a quarterback named Johnny Unitas who was as good a passer as anybody in the

National Football League and they ought to give him a tryout. (Weeb Ewbank always used to tell everybody I wrote the letter myself.)

I think the truth is that the whole series of events started right after the Steelers cut me, when I wrote to Coach Camp at Louisville and told him what had happened and asked him to give me a boost to any pro scout or coach he might run into. "I know you're not interested in excuses," I told him, "but I want to give you the facts. I don't feel the Steelers gave me any kind of an opportunity at all." Camp believed me, and he still had faith in me himself, so when he got a chance to build me up to Weeb Ewbank, whom he had played against in college, he did his best for me. Actually, Camp had talked to Weeb about me while I was still in school, and like the Browns, the Colts had had me down for a possible late pick in the 1955 draft if nobody else took me. Now, because all they had at quarterback was George Shaw and Gary Kerkorian, and Kerkorian had already told them he was going to quit and go to law school, they were coming after me. Thank God.

Weeb and I got along fine right from the time I went through that workout for him in the spring and he said I would do and told Kellett to give me a contract and assign me a room in training camp. I would have got along with the meanest man in the world if he was giving me a chance to make the National League, but Weeb Ewbank was everything a worried rookie could ask for in a coach.

Right from the beginning he spent time with me, talked with me, watched me, criticized me, offered suggestions to me, and in every way acted as though he considered me a part of his football team. After my experience with the Steelers, it was a brand-new world, and the best part of it was that I was made to feel that I belonged in it. I think about the only thing Weeb and I didn't agree on, and we never did agree on it all through the seven seasons I played for him, was the way I threw short passes.

46

He thought I threw them too hard, and I thought they ought to be thrown hard. I've never liked to lob passes. They may be easy to catch but they're also easy to intercept, and anything that's easy to intercept I don't like. But even though he thought George Shaw had it all over me when it came to throwing the short ones, Weeb gave me credit for being a good long passer. He also gave me a chance, which was what I needed.

My first big shot came in the intrasquad game the Colts put on for their fans every year in Memorial Stadium just before we leave training camp to start the preseason games. Admission to the game is a dollar a person, no tickets are printed, and it's first come, first served for the seats. The money goes to charity, and it's a good tradition. The fans get a chance to look over the new ball club, take pictures, collect autographs, and get their throats in shape for yelling their way through the season. There were more than 38,000 of them there for my first game, a pretty good crowd for an intrasquad game, and they made a lot of noise for the familiar faces, Gino Marchetti, Bill Pellington, Alan Ameche, Art Donovan, Steve Myhra, L. G. Dupre, Buzz Nutter, Bert Rechichar, Alex Sandusky, Art Spinney, and all the others.

They saw some pretty good early-season football, too, with Shaw quarterbacking one team and me the other in a 20–20 tie. George completed seven passes for a hundred yards and one touchdown and was also the top ball carrier in the game with forty-three yards in five carries. I completed fourteen passes for 288 yards and two touchdowns, and I scored one touchdown myself on a quarterback sneak from one yard out.

Weeb Ewbank said some nice things about me after the game. "One thing about the way this boy throws the long ones," he told a reporter in one story that Dorothy pasted in her new scrapbook, "is that he isn't satisfied just to get the ball down there and hope somebody will be able to run fast enough and far enough to get to it. That's what a lot of quarterbacks do. But not Unitas. He waits until his man has a good start downfield, then he measures the target and lets fly with the intention of putting the ball right in the man's hands. It's no accident when he does it. He means to do it, believe me."

I felt even better about a story the Baltimore *Sun* ran with the headline UNITAS SEEN NO. 2 COLT QUARTERBACK. The story said: "If the Colts were to open their 1956 National Football League campaign tomorrow, Johnny Unitas would be their No. 2 quarterback—and not by default. Unitas, who had a brief trial with Pittsburgh a year ago, and incumbent George Shaw are the only signal callers in camp. But the way Johnny has gone about his duties, a casual observer would be led to believe that the field general corps was suffering from overpopulation. So well has the newcomer done in overall performance that even if Gary Kerkorian, who ran behind Shaw last season, were present, he might not be able to outlast the rookie from Louisville U."

That was what I wanted to hear. I knew I still had a long way to go before I began to collect any of that $7,000 I would get if I survived the last cut. I also knew that if the club decided they needed Kerkorian back badly enough to offer him a good big raise, they could probably get him to change his mind. So I wasn't taking anything for granted, and every kind word was welcome. I remember a few days before the intrasquad game John Steadman, who is the sports editor of the *News-American* now but who was the publicity director of the Colts in 1956, taped an interview with me to use in promoting the exhibition game we were going to play with the Eagles in Louisville on September 9. I kidded him about it when we made it. "Do you really think I'll still be here then?" I asked him.

The day after the intrasquad game, Steadman stopped by my room at Western Maryland and said, in his quiet way, "I think we'll be able to use that recording all right, John."

They did use it, too, and we drew more than 20,000 people and a gate of about $70,000 for the game in Louisville. It was a break for me that the game was on the schedule because, as a concession to the fact that I had played my college ball there, they started me at quarterback. It was one more chance, and I did my best to make the most of it.

Right after that game Kellett called me in and told me Weeb wanted me for his backup quarterback and the club was going to put me on the official roster. My pay, like everybody else's, wouldn't start until we opened the season, but I could call myself a professional football player at last. It was strictly up to me to prove that I deserved to be one.

I didn't do much work for my money in the first few games. Shaw was at his best in our opening game. We beat the Bears, 28–21, and George had a great day with nineteen completions in twenty-five attempts for 231 yards. He hit on fourteen out of his first fifteen passes. It's hard to do much better than that, and nobody needed me to do anything except sit on the bench and be ready in case George broke a leg or something. But a couple of weeks later, after we had lost two games in a row to the Lions and the Packers, he almost did just that, and I suddenly found myself in business.

We were playing the Bears for the second time, and George hurt his knee badly when he was buried in a heavy pileup. It never pays to be buried in a pileup by the Bears, and it didn't pay for George this time. A year later, even after an operation, his knee still wasn't the same. For me, of course, the injury was the opportunity of a lifetime. The club had nobody except me, and it was up to me to do the job.

Weeb must have had some bad moments when I took over that first time. We were right in the ball game when George had to leave, and when Carl Taseff grabbed the ball on a short field-goal try and took it ninety-six yards down the field for a touchdown, we went ahead, 21–20. But we didn't stay ahead very long. J. C. Caroline intercepted one of my passes and ran it back for a touchdown, and I messed up a couple of handoffs that caused fumbles and gave the Bears easy touchdowns. We got beat, 58–27, and if you wanted to be kind you could have said it wasn't all my fault, but if you wanted to be accurate you had to say that I was responsible for a good part of it. Weeb tried to make me feel better by telling me that it's hard to come off the bench cold like that, and that because we hadn't worked together enough yet, the guys in the backfield had been bumping into me just as much as I had been bumping into them. But I knew I had been no ball of fire.

I was lucky there was nobody else the club could put in there for our next game, with the Packers. I kept hearing that Kellett was trying to get Kerkorian to come back, but he hadn't come back yet, and even if he did, there was no way he could get ready to play the next ball game. That one would be mine, even if I never had another one.

Weeb did everything he could to get me ready. He had me run plays with the regular backs, Ameche, Moore and Dupre, all week. He had me throw to our prime receivers, Mutscheller, Berry and Moore. He talked over everything we planned to do and everything he thought we might run into. He told me what he expected of me and he said he knew I could get the job done. The way it turned out, we did all right. I threw the ball sixteen times and connected with eight, two of them good for touchdowns. My handoffs were a whole lot better, after all that hard work, and the best thing I did all day was to keep handing the ball to Lenny Moore. Lenny ran thirteen times for 185 yards, including two sensational touchdown runs of seventy-two and seventy-nine yards. We won the game, 28–21, and Weeb told me I had done all right. I didn't even mind when the word came down that Kerkorian was coming back, especially when Weeb told me he was coming back as number two quarterback, not number one. Until either Shaw had two sound knees again or I fell apart at the seams, the job was mine.

The next game was a big one for me because it meant so much to the coach. We were taking on the Browns in Cleveland,

and Weeb, who had put in five years as Paul Brown's assistant before he got the Baltimore job, and who hadn't left Paul on the best of terms, wanted this one badly. Because we're in different divisions, we get to play the Browns in a regular-season game only once every six or seven years. The only other way we ever get a shot at them is in a World's Championship game. Weeb didn't want to miss this chance, and whatever he wanted, I wanted.

The Browns scored first, mostly because our line couldn't stop Ed Modzelewski, the Maryland All-America they called Big Mo. His brother, Dick Modzelewski, is Little Mo, not because he is little but because he is younger than Ed. We got a chance to tie it up when the Browns fumbled on their own thirty-five. I went back to pass, but it looked as if the whole Cleveland team was coming in on me, so I took off with the ball and made it down to the one-yard line before they caught up with me. The Browns were offside on the next play and were penalized half the distance to the goal line. I gave the ball to Ameche and he went over for the touchdown. We made the kick and it was 7–7, which was the way it stayed until the last quarter. The break came when Gino Marchetti red-dogged Babe Parilli on a pass play and knocked the ball right out of his hand when he hit him. Doug Eggers was there to fall on it, and we had possession on our own forty-two. Paul Brown and the Cleveland players were pretty unhappy about the officials' call on the fumble. They thought that Parilli had got the ball away and that Gino had just knocked it down and it should have been ruled an incomplete pass. But the ruling stood, as rulings almost always do, and we had the ball.

We were called for holding on the first play from scrimmage, which put the ball back on our twenty-seven. I figured they would be looking for a pass to make up the yardage, so I gave the ball to Moore, and Lenny, with that great fluid running style of his, went all the way for the touchdown, seventy-three yards of the prettiest broken-field running you ever saw in your life. Then, as now, when Lenny has his health, there is nobody who can touch him. With the kick, we had a 14–7 lead, but we all knew that wasn't likely to be enough, and we went after more with everything we had. We got the ball away from the Browns in midfield by knocking down four straight passes and taking over on their forty-six. Ameche took it to the eleven for us, Dupre made three more, we lost five yards for taking too much time in the huddle, got back two of them on a short pass to Mutscheller, and then Dupre went off tackle for the touchdown that made Weeb Ewbank the happiest coach in the National Football League.

You got some idea of the way Brown and Ewbank played that one from the picture the newspapers printed the next day of Paul Brown walking off the field with his head down and his hands in his pockets. He didn't even give Weeb a nod. Not that Weeb cared. He had proved that he could put together a pretty good football team without any help from the great man, and he was satisfied.

That was the game that put me over the hump. Even though Kerkorian did come back, there never was any talk about him going in ahead of me. And by the time Shaw was ready again, I had the job to keep. It just goes to prove that in a league like this one it doesn't pay to get hurt and stay out for any length of time. There are too many good men around to take our place. As Satchel Paige, the pitcher, always used to say, "Never look back. Somebody may be gaining on you."

I like to think that I was able to pay back a little of what I owed Weeb in the last game of the season. The word was out all over town that Weeb's job was on the block and that the boss, Carroll Rosenbloom, had pretty much decided to fire him but wasn't going to make up his mind finally until the season was officially over. The reporters all concluded that it was win or else for Weeb in our last game, at Washington, and all of us on the ball club made up our minds we weren't going to blow the coach's job for him if we could help it.

It didn't look too good for Weeb for a long time. We were losing, 17–12, with only a few minutes left in the ball game. But we had the ball, and we kept trying. I threw a long one from midfield to Jim Mutscheller, who reached for it on the five-yard line. Norb Hecker of the Redskins deflected the ball over Jim's head, but Jim didn't give up on it. He lunged backward for it, grabbed it, and carried it over the line with what looked like half the Washington team hanging onto him. The kick was good, we had the ball game, 19–17, and the next day Carroll Rosenbloom announced that Weeb would be back in 1957.

Both of them, Carroll and Weeb, told me I would be back, too. The Colts haven't got rid of me yet. Maybe if I keep going to church every chance I get, they won't.

CHAPTER THREE

IF YOU'RE A QUARTERBACK in the National Football League, the main thing you've got to be able to do for your keep is throw the ball. You've got to handle it well, too, of course. You've got to know how to fake. You've got to make your hand-offs on running plays firmly and surely, so that the ball doesn't get dropped all over the backfield. You've got to know how to call the plays, unless you want to leave all of that to the coach —and no coach on the sidelines can do as good a job of calling a game as a quarterback who sees what's going on out there and knows how to take advantage of it. It helps if you can run a little, because you run away from a lot of fifteen-yard losses if you're quick on your feet and you can also (as Y. A. Tittle did for years with that bootleg play of his) run over a few touch-downs for yourself. And it isn't going to make anybody mad if you learn how to throw a good hard block. But the thing you get paid for is throwing the ball.

I grip the ball with the last two fingers of my right hand on the laces. The rest of my hand is behind the laces. If the ball is wet I move a couple more fingers right up on the laces, to get a better grip on it. The grip, of course, is the most important single factor in passing, and the manufacturers don't help us quarterbacks any with that smooth finish they put on the ball. Some of the new footballs they give us in the National League are just like glass. They look pretty, but they are hard to throw. The worst of them all, though, are the night balls. Fortunately, we usually see them only during the preseason schedule, although we did play a night game in Baltimore against the St. Louis Cardinals in October 1964, because the park in St. Louis, where the game was supposed to be played, was being used by the baseball Cardinals and the Yankees for the World Series, and when the game was rescheduled for Baltimore they made it at night so it wouldn't conflict with the television of the Series.

I hate that night ball. They paint those white stripes on it down near the end of the ball, right where I grip it with the three fingers that have the most to do with throwing the ball. The paint they make those lines out of shines like enamel, and it is as slippery as the devil. I'm all right if I can fool around with the balls for a few days before one of those preseason games and sort of scuff them up a little, but when I have to take a brand-new one and throw it, I never know whether it's going to go end-over-end or what.

As with everything else, you've got to practice passing all the time. We hang a net between the goal posts to stop the ball and I stand out there and throw to all of our receivers for at least half an hour every day. One of the things I practice a lot is throwing behind the receiver, making him come back for the ball. When you see one of those in a game it may look like a bad pass but it may actually be perfect. Looks don't count. It's keeping the ball away from the defender's hands and putting it into the receiver's that counts.

You've always got to think about the defender, what he can do and can't do, as well as about the receiver, what his personal likes, dislikes, and abilities are. There are a million things to consider before you put the ball up in the air. Some receivers like to have the ball come at them from left to right, some from right to left. Some are very good at catching the ball way out in front, reaching with their fingertips, and some can catch it only if you throw it right in on their chests. Some defenders search a receiver like a pickpocket going through your pockets, and some go at him like a prizefighter who has his man on the ropes and isn't going to let him get away. As much as possible, you've got to keep all of these things in mind and try to use what you know, just the way a baseball pitcher uses what he knows about all the hitters in the league—and also about all the men behind him in the field.

The receiver has to do his part, too. He can't just run out there and let you worry about getting the ball to him. Jimmy Orr explained it this way one time on a television show: "You have to learn how to shake yourself loose. That's an art that every new pro has to learn from scratch, because he didn't have to learn it in college. There, you just run for an open place. Up here you have to learn the moves, because there ain't any open places."

As I said, I favor a hard pass whenever I can throw one. But naturally it varies according to the situation. Hard passes are safer because it's tough for the defense to intercept them, but on the other hand you can't throw bullets when you're up close to the receiver. Nobody could catch them. The speed with which the ball ought to be thrown at a given distance is something that you can work out for yourself by hours and hours of practice with your receivers. It isn't as tedious as it sounds. I like to throw the ball, and men like Raymond Berry, who I think is the best receiver in the business, and Jimmy Orr and Lenny Moore and John Mackey and Tony Lorick like to run and catch it. We also like to win on Sunday afternoon, and we know the best way to make sure we do is to practice and practice and practice.

I can throw the ball with pretty fair accuracy between fifty and sixty yards, but I seldom do throw it that far in a game. You hardly ever throw more than thirty-five or forty yards, at the most. By the time the receiver is twenty or twenty-five yards downfield, you've got to get rid of the ball. Of course, if he has run that far when you throw it, you've got to lead him with the pass another fifteen or twenty yards, so the ball may be in the air about forty yards on the average long pass. You hardly ever have time to let your man get so far downfield before you throw the ball that it goes as much as fifty yards in the air.

When I go back to throw I don't worry about the linemen coming in on me, only about what the linebackers and the secondary are doing. Once you start worrying about the linemen you're not going to be looking downfield at your receivers and at the defenders the way you should. You're not going to be doing your job, and all that means is that they're going to put somebody in there who will do it.

My protection is good. It was better in 1964 than it had been any time since we last won the championship, in 1959. They don't come any better at bodyguarding the quarterback than big Jim Parker. He has saved me many a ride on the seat of my pants. I may have to get rid of the ball a little faster than I did back in '58 and '59, but not much. I remember telling a reporter during the '59 season that if I got hit nine or ten times in a game, that was a lot. Well, I might have been getting hit a little more often in the years in between, but with the personnel we've got at Baltimore now, I would say I'm back to where I was in those good years. You have to remember that sometimes, when I'm hit back there, it isn't the fault of my protection at all. It stands to reason that if you're going to hang onto the ball until the last second, the way I do, you're going to have to eat it once in a while. I like to wait until the last gasp to get it away. I get dropped a lot more that way, but I complete a lot more passes, too, and that's what I get paid for.

Some writers have asked me if I get hit more in practice now that Don Shula has got rid of the red shirt Weeb Ewbank used to make me wear. Ed Linn once wrote a story about that red shirt. "When the Baltimore Colts hold a practice session," he said, "the squad is divided into three parts. The offensive players wear white jerseys, the defensive players wear blue jerseys, and the third force, consisting of Johnny Unitas, wears a faded red sweatshirt. Unitas does not wear the red sweatshirt because of any personal superstition or because of any desire on the part of the club to make things easy for the spectators. The red sweatshirt is a signal for his teammates to break stride when they come within trampling distance of him. Baltimore is not anxious to have any of its infantrymen bruise football's top passer by mistaking him for just another of the troops."

I try to explain to the writers that it doesn't make any difference, the guys aren't going to go out of their way to knock me down in practice no matter what color shirt I'm wearing. It was just an idea Weeb had. Shula doesn't want anybody hitting me unnecessarily, either. He just doesn't go for red shirts, that's all.

As far as my protection is concerned, I've played nine seasons in the National Football League and I haven't lost a tooth yet, so it must be pretty good. Of course, it wouldn't make any difference how good it was if I didn't use it, so I make pretty sure I stay inside the pocket as long as the pocket is there. I know the fans like to watch a scrambling quarterback, the kind, for instance, George Mira was in college and still was when he came up with the Forty-Niners in 1964. It's exciting to see the man with the ball dodging around out there while all those monsters try to grab him, but it's not good football. It's fine for you to be able to do that when you have to, but you should never run around back there while you've still got blockers on their feet able to protect you. A rollout is different, of course, but the quarterback who is going to have a good record of completions is the quarterback who stays inside his pocket and spends his time looking downfield instead of playing leapfrog with a bunch of blitzers.

Mira, incidentally, is going to make a real good quarterback. He's got a good arm, and he's quick. He's been used to throwing the low, bullet pass all the time, and he will have to learn to loop the ball a little more up here to keep it away from the defenders, but I have no doubt he will learn that, just as he will learn that you're a lot better off staying with your protection than you are running away from it.

What I hope to get from my blockers is a minimum of two and a half seconds in which to get rid of the ball. If I get three seconds, I'm in pretty good shape, because my receiver has had fifteen or twenty yards in which to beat his man and break open. Also, I have had enough time to fake a pass before throwing the real one, which is important, because no matter how well you can throw the ball you aren't going to get very far unless you can fool the defense. You've got to give the defense three or four different things to worry about, not just one. If they're pretty sure they know what the receivers are going to do and what you're going to do, they can get themselves all set to pick it off. So it's up to you to make sure they can't guess accurately, or if you think they have, it's up to you to check off your play at the line of scrimmage and cross them up.

Say I've had Raymond Berry run a couple of inside moves, and maybe on the last one the defensive man actually got a hand on the ball. I'll tell Raymond in the huddle, "All right, this time we'll run an outside pass off an inside move." Don't forget, we've already caught a few on this man inside, and maybe he's overplaying Raymond a little bit, which is just what we want. So we line up and I get the ball and go back with it. At about twelve yards out, Raymond will cut as though he's really coming inside, and if I have time I'll give a short pumping motion in his direction. The defensive backs always play the quarterback's eyes and follow the movement of the ball, and if I can get the defender to overplay him as I pump, Raymond can watch for him to commit himself and then bust outside, and it's wide open there for him. But all of this depends on whether or not you have enough time back there.

Unless your pocket of protection holds together long enough, you can't waste any time on fakes. You have all you can do to throw the ball and hope you're throwing it where it won't be intercepted. But for us to run a pass pattern the way we like to run it, I've got to have time to fake a little. Say I have a side-line pass on, and I'm thinking mainly to my right side because the way the defensive man is playing he is giving us the side line. For protection I've got four linemen, the center, and two backs blocking. That's seven men. Then I have three receivers, the flanker, the tight end and the split end. I've called the side-line pass specifically because I want to hit the flanker, who probably is Jimmy Orr. As I come up to the line of scrimmage I can see that the defense is going to rotate, in an attempt to shut me off from the sideline pass. Watching the defenders just as closely as I watch my receivers, I try to figure out where the next possible receiver, beyond the flanker, will break open. Our pass patterns call for our first receiver to break at about ten yards, so my next logical choice would be the tight end, who ought to come open at about twelve yards. If he doesn't make it I've got to look for my outside end, the split end, who should be coming open at about fifteen or eighteen yards. So as I drop back with the ball, and see the defense rotate into a zone, I know right away that my side-line pass is out. There's no possible way that we can hit with it. And I know it's going to take the outside end a little bit longer to get open because he has to go deeper. But he's my logical second choice, so, as I set myself with the ball, gripping it with my right hand and shielding it with my left hand for extra protection, I pump in the direction of the tight end, who is breaking open at twelve yards. He may be covered like a tent, but I pump toward him anyway because I must have time for the outside end to shake loose.

When you pump, most halfbacks—defensive halfbacks—have a tendency to relax just a little bit if they see that you're not looking in their direction when your arm begins the pumping motion. They figure you're throwing, and not in their direction, which means the play is over as far as they're concerned and they can take it a little easy. Which is just what you want. You pump for the fake to the tight end, then you come right back to the outside end. If you have run the pattern right and pulled off a believable fake, you are going to catch the defender slacking off just enough so that, bing, you hit your man for a good fifteen yards.

If the defensive line has been giving you a bad time with a rush, one of your best weapons to fight back with is the screen pass. Your blocking is set up the same way as usual, but your men don't hold as long as they try to do on a regular pass. They will count, like maybe, a thousand-one, a thousand-two, and then they will let their man go, act like they are really beaten. The quarterback sets up at his regular passing distance at first, then, as these guys start coming in on you, you go back another ten yards gradually and then throw out to the side to one of your backs. In the meantime your linemen have got up and gone out in front of the back who is catching the ball, and if you're in luck, it's straight down the sideline for a big gain.

You use the screen not just for the gain you may be able to get out of that particular play but also because it helps you set up your pass protection. If you hit them with a couple of good screens, the line that has been rushing you so hard won't be able to keep coming in like that. They have to hit and look at the same time and be ready to pull back if necessary. It's true that the secondary usually can make the tackle soon after the man catches the screen pass, but sometimes the blocking is there and the man gets away, and anyway a few good screens can eat up a lot of yardage. They have to be concerned about it, and as soon as you've got them worrying, you have succeeded in taking something off their rush.

I've always made a specialty of the long pass, the bomb, which has the same double payoff for you that the home run does in baseball. You not only get the big gain, or the score, but you also shake up the other team, you hurt their confidence, you put a lot of extra pressure on them. I will go for the long one anytime a man tells me on the way into the huddle (I don't let anybody open his mouth once we get into the huddle) that he can beat his man deep or anytime I think myself that the defensive man is playing one of our receivers extra tight and that our man probably can get behind him. Sometimes I will throw deep even when I know it's not going to be there, when I'm pretty sure we aren't going to complete it. I'll do it just to worry them, just to give them something else to think about. I always want them to know that we are willing to go deep. I don't want them ever thinking that they can play our receivers tight. The more I throw deep, the better my chances are of completing the short ones. I often throw one way out there on the first play of the game, just for the effect it has on them. If you complete that one, it's just like the first batter up in the ball game hitting the first pitch out of the park. But even if you don't complete it, you've made sure the defense is going to stay loose for a while and not zero in on you the way they might if they didn't have to worry about a long one.

It's the old principle that you throw according to what the defense does. The defensive linemen will tell you, as soon as you go back with the ball, who you're going to throw to. They don't want to tell you, but they do. It's up to you to take advantage of it, not only to complete your passes, but also to avoid interceptions. Throws that you make too quickly, off balance, without looking carefully, without checking the defense as carefully as you check your receivers, are good candidates for interception. I always figure that an interception has one of three basic causes: a poorly run pattern, a hard charge by the linemen that makes the quarterback throw the ball just to get rid of it, or a plain ordinary miserable throw.

Of all the bad things a quarterback can do, throwing the ball just to get rid of it is probably the worst. It's an easy habit to get into, because you don't like to take that loss of seven, eight or ten yards all the time, but you're better off doing that than throwing the ball up for grabs. Sometimes you can't help it, like when a lineman comes charging in on you with his hands up in the air and deflects the ball just enough so that it hangs up there for anybody to grab it. That's just one of those things. But a poor choice of receivers is your fault, and it can be avoided if you study your personnel and the personnel of the other team and go into the ball game knowing what patterns and what receivers are most likely to work for you, and what moves by which receivers are most likely to give you trouble.

Interceptions are the worst sin a quarterback can commit, because the main thing you have to do to win a football game is control the ball. Whenever you give the ball up it's hard to come by again, but when you give it up on an interception you're not only giving up possession but also a lot of yardage —and you can't afford to do it very often. Generally speaking, a quarterback in the National Football League is doing all right if he keeps his interceptions down below one a game for the fourteen games on the schedule. Obviously, when you throw the ball almost 300 times in a season, you're bound to get a few of them picked off. But you had better keep it down to a few.

I hold a few National Football League passing records that I'm proud of, especially the one I set in 1963 for the Most Passes Completed, Season, 237. I consider that particular statistic the most important goal for a quarterback, because he isn't going to be able to move his team very well unless he can throw the ball successfully and consistently. I hold another record that may last a long time, for throwing touchdown passes in the most consecutive games, forty-seven, which I did between the seasons of 1956 and 1960. That's the kind of record, like Joe DiMaggio's consecutive-game hitting streak, that requires a lot of luck and a lot of help from other people. To give you an idea, the record I broke, Cecil Isbell's, was twenty-two, and it was established back in 1941 and 1942. It lasted for sixteen years. I'm second to Sonny Jurgensen in yards gained in one season. Sonny had 3,723 in 1961 and I had 3,481 in 1963. And I'm second to Y.A. Tittle for the most touchdown passes in one season. Y.A. had thirty-six in 1963 and I had thirty-two in 1959. But the record I would most like to have is the one for the fewest passes intercepted in a season. I covet that one. Roman Gabriel holds it with a miraculous two for the Rams in 1962. He only threw the ball 101 times that season, and I have thrown as many as 420 passes in a single season. But to give you an idea of what even a busy quarterback can accomplish, Charlie Conerly had only four interceptions out of 194 passes in 1959. Anyway, it's a record I'll keep trying for. Generally the last thing Dorothy says to me before a game is, "Good luck, and no interceptions." She knows what's important.

The sideline pass is a good way to avoid interceptions, because if you throw it right it will go safely out of bounds if your receiver doesn't catch it. Another way to prevent them is the checkoff, or automatic, where you change the play at the line of scrimmage. If a quarterback works for a coach who calls all of the plays from the bench, the way Paul Brown used to do for the Cleveland Browns, there are no automatics. And, in my opinion, the quarterback is in trouble, and so is the team. But most pro ball clubs use them when they have to, which is whenever you get up over the ball and see that the way the defense has set up they are going to kill you if you go through with the play you called in the huddle.

I begin calling all of my plays with a color, one of six we use in each game. We always have three "live" colors and three "dead" ones, or decoys. The play I call in the huddle may be "Fifty right, on two," which means a pass play in our fifty series, the ball to be snapped on the count of two. When we line up, if I think the play ought to have a good chance against the way the defense has set up, I will start my call with one of the dead colors. If the dead colors for the day are red, white and blue, I may call, "Red, fifty, hut one, hut two" —and the center will stuff the ball in my hands with the laces exactly where I always hold the ball for throwing, and we're in business. If, on the other hand, the defense has set up in a way that makes me think we can't possibly go with the play I had planned, I will start my call with one of the live colors, which may be black, yellow and green. As soon as I say "Green," my teammates know we're switching to an automatic, and they wait for me to identify the new play. They know the ball will still be snapped on two, so the count remains the same.

A lot of nonsense is written about automatics. They are made, sometimes, to sound like a magic way to mix up the other team and exploit subtle weaknesses that the brilliant quarterback has been able to spot in the defense. Actually, automatics carry a lot of risk. When you call a play in the huddle, the players have had time to think about it, to go over in their minds exactly what they are supposed to do, and by the time you go up over the ball, they are ready to do it. When you throw that play away and call an automatic, they've got only a second or two in which to switch over mentally to what they have to do now. Generally speaking, you're better off sticking to the play you called in the huddle. But not, of course, when you know that, either because of guessing right

65

or because of just plain luck, the defense is fixed to stop your play cold. Then you must have the freedom to change, even if the play you are going to throw out happens to be one the coach sent in.

I don't check off as much as I used to a few years ago. We're using the type of formations now that almost dictate what the defense has to do, so there is usually not much point in checking off. I don't think I did it more than four or five times a game in 1964. We have a good idea of what the defense will do against our different formations, and we're ready for it, or think we are, so I change it only when they come up with something completely different and I'm convinced that the play I had in mind can't possibly go. And, of course, the defense can always check off at the same time. It's all a big guessing game out there. Mostly I try to stick to what I have believed in ever since I was playing high-school football, that I've got to have a good reason for every play I call. You just don't pick something out and call it for the sake of calling it. You don't pull plays out of a hat. You build from one play to another, you have something in mind all the time. In this league you had better have or you are going to be in bad shape.

The big thing about tactics is the element of surprise. You have to avoid typing yourself. That means you can't always call your plays by the book, but it also means—and I had to learn this the hard way—that you can't call the offbeat play all the time either. I know I typed myself back in 1956 and 1957 just as surely by calling the surprise play all the time as I would have by calling the book play. When I had a third down and short yardage situation, I would throw the ball, figuring they would surely be looking for a run. After a while, my unorthodox play calling became just as bad for me as strictly orthodox calling might be for another quarterback. I was forgetting to mix them up, and it didn't take the defense long to figure me out. They would be so sure that I would pass on that third-down situation that they would play loose and lay back for the pass and be in great position to knock it down or intercept it. It was stupid, and I finally saw from the movies what I was doing and put a stop to it. Ever since, I've kept it firmly in mind that you can't afford to let your play calling become predictable. Sometimes you have to go away from a play you would really like to call in this particular situation just because you know you can gain more by shaking them up with something they have made up their minds you wouldn't even consider doing. It can pay big dividends for you later in the ball game. The best thing that can happen to a quarterback is for him to get the reputation that you never know what he's going to do next.

The looseness and the flexibility of the tactics they use up here is one of the main differences between college football and pro football. College football, I always say, is strictly three yards and a cloud of dust. Whereas in college you generally have only a couple of outstanding players on each team, in pro ball every man who plays regularly is outstanding. He has not only size but also speed, and as a result you can open up more and try different things. It's true that the professional game is about sixty percent passing, for the very reason that with such fine players out there against you on defense, it's hard to run with the ball successfully. But that other forty percent is what keeps the game honest and makes it interesting. If you knew that every play was going to be a pass, it would get pretty monotonous. In college ball you pretty well know that almost every play is going to be a run, and that's just as bad, or worse.

You've got to keep the other team off balance—that's the whole secret of football. If you're all pass, they play you that way, rushing the passer and crowding the receivers. The line backers lay back and wait. If you're all run, they play you that way, massing tight to gang up on the blockers and the ball carrier. The line backers come in fast, and they kill you.

You have to mix up the plays, run Tony Lorick one way and Lenny Moore another, and throw the ball when they expect you to and when they don't expect you to, so that they don't dare commit themselves until the last second. That's when it may be too late.

Like all pro quarterbacks, I always sit by the bench phones when I'm out of the game. Don McCaffrey, our assistant back-field coach, sits upstairs during the game and spots from there, and when he sees something he thinks I ought to know about, he calls me up and tells me about it. Sometimes I will have something I want him to check out for me, like whether or not one of their men is playing a little out of position, and I will call him. When I'm not by the phones I will be standing on the sidelines next to Don Shula, talking things over. If there is anything wrong with me physically I try to have Eddie Block, the trainer, or Dr. Ed McDonald, who is one of the best ortho-pedic men in the country, take care of it before we get the ball back and it's time to go again. I've been lucky that in all my time in the league, I have had only one serious injury, a punc-tured lung and three broken ribs, which I got against the Packers in 1958. People are always asking me if it isn't danger-ous playing quarterback in the NFL, if the other teams don't try to get you, but all I can say is that I've never been played dirty. Never. After all, I have been at it for a long time and not only have I, as I said, never lost a tooth, but the only game I ever missed was the one the week after I got hurt that time. I've been hit hard, been beat up a lot, but always legally. I've been hit in the face, sure, but only with a legal shoulder or arm or helmet. I have never been punched.

I might say I don't go around punching anybody, either. I've never been in a fight on the field. I'm not big enough to be fighting anybody in this game. I'm not going to pick on some-body who's anywhere from 240 to 280, I can tell you that. Anytime they start fighting out there, I just stand around and watch. It's different in baseball, you know. Hardly anybody ever gets hurt in those baseball fights, but in football, guys are a little too big, and sometimes they get pretty heated up out there because of all that close contact work. The best thing for a guy my size to do when those big fellows get mad is just mind my own business, and that's what I do. If I keep on doing it, maybe I can stick around, calling the plays and throwing the ball, as long as Y. A. Tittle did.

CHAPTER FOUR

T HE GAMES at Memorial Stadium in Baltimore start at two o'clock on Sunday afternoon and generally are over not much after half past four. But the game begins, for me, when I leave the house at about half past eight Saturday night, and it doesn't really end until Dorothy and I pull into the garage along about midnight Sunday.

The weekend of November 1, 1964, when we played the Forty-Niners at home, was a typical one. We ate dinner on Saturday at about six o'clock. We had some friends in from out of town, and Dorothy made a big casserole of lasagna. With it we had a bowlful of mixed green salad, for which everybody fixed his own dressing—Roquefort, French, or oil and vinegar. It was Halloween, and for dessert Dorothy gave us pumpkin pie. Some of the people put whipped cream on top of the pie but I decided I could do without that. The neighborhood trick-or-treaters kept ringing the doorbell, and we admired their costumes and tried to guess who they were. I didn't even recognize my own little girl, Janice Ann, who was made up like Ringo Starr, right down to a red Beatle wig and a black bowler hat. What with all the excitement, we just about had time to drink our coffee before it was half past eight, time for me to leave for town.

Don Shula thinks it helps to have us check in at a motel at nine o'clock the night before each home game and stay there until it's time to leave for the ball park in the morning. He thinks we get a better night's rest that way, with nobody to bother us. There is a lot of difference of opinion as far as that's concerned, but the only opinion that counts is Shula's, so we spend the night in the motel. I said goodbye to everybody, kissed Dorothy at the door (she said I ought to get mad at her about something because when I leave the house mad we always win), and took off for the Castle Motor Inn, a trip that takes me about twenty minutes on the Beltway, driving easily in my gold Pontiac. (I don't actually own the Pontiac; I get a new one from the company every year, on a promotional deal, and I hope they keep on thinking it's a good idea to have me drive one, because I think it's a very good idea.)

As the other ballplayers came in, we sat around the motel and talked football and went over our plans for the ball game. Then we had a small steak and a bottle of beer, went to our rooms and watched television for a while, and were asleep by midnight.

I made eight o'clock Mass at St. Jude's Church, which is about a block from the motel, read the Sunday papers, and was in the dining room for the team breakfast at ten o'clock. Compared with some of the other guys I'm not what you would call a big eater, but I'm good for juice and a couple of eggs with bacon and toast and coffee. That always holds me until dinner after the game. Right after breakfast we assembled for a meeting with the coaches that lasted until eleven, and then I went back to my own room with my play book and got myself as ready as I could get. One of the things Shula had done at the meeting was to give me the three plays he wanted me to use on our first offensive series, and I went over them with special care. All the coaches work hard on those three plays, trying to come up with something that will get us off to a good start. It's a pet idea of Shula's, having the three plays set before the game, and I think it's a good one. I always run them off just as we've planned unless something goes seriously wrong.

At a quarter of twelve I left the motel and drove to the stadium. We've often talked about going to the stadium in a bus, but we all want to have our cars there for after the game, so we prefer going on our own. When I got there, I went in to the trainer's room and got a rubdown and had my ankles taped, and after that it was just the regular bull session. Everybody has his own way of showing that he is nervous. Some guys talk a lot and others won't say two words. There are always a couple of guys being funny. Like Jim Parker. He made believe he was Carroll Rosenbloom giving us a pep talk.

After a while I started the business of getting ready for the game. Sometimes I have a rubdown, and sometimes, if I feel real good, I don't bother. That day, I wanted one because I felt a little tight in the back and the shoulders. So I spent half an hour being rubbed, having my ankles taped, and listening to Dimitri Spassoff, Eddie Block's assistant, going through one of his monologues. Then I got dressed up to the waist, and after that I staked out the trainer's table and lay down until it was time to finish getting dressed.

It was one o'clock when I got up and found somebody to help me pull my jersey down over my shoulder pads, which is the hardest thing we have to do to get ready to play. At a quarter past one I picked up a football and asked Bobby Boyd to throw it back and forth with me, to warm up, right in the locker room. I guess we kept that up for fifteen or twenty minutes, and then it was close enough to game time for us all to just sort of settle down and wait. Shula talked to us a little before we went out on the field, about what we knew about them and what we knew about ourselves, and then it was time to go. I was just beginning to get a little nervous when they told us to go out there.

The officials tossed the coin for the two captains in a corner of the field while the rest of us were running through plays and loosening up. They always go through the coin-tossing bit in the middle of the field just before the kickoff when the game is on television, but that's strictly for the camera. Actually it has already been done off in the corner where nobody can see it. Somebody has won and has decided who is going to kick off to whom and who is going to defend which goal.

The Forty-Niners won the toss this time and we kicked off to them. They couldn't move the ball and had to kick to us. We were so glad to get our hands on the ball that we moved it sixty-eight yards for a touchdown on six plays, the last one a twenty-yard pass from me to Raymond Berry. The Forty-Niners blocked Lou Michaels' place kick for the point after touchdown, but we were ahead 6–0, and we stayed ahead for the rest of the ball game. We made it 9–0 with a field goal late in the first quarter, and then 23–0 at the half. Steve Stonebreaker picked a John Brodie fumble out of the air and ran into the end zone with it, and Lenny Moore took the ball over from the two at the end of a long drive that we started on our own sixteen.

When we went into the locker room, the defense took over one end of the room and the offense the other. The scouts we had up in the press box during the game, trying to spot holes in the Forty-Niners' defense for us, started right in on the blackboard. They told us what we had been doing offensively that was good, what we hadn't been doing that we ought to try, and what we had been doing that hadn't been working and that we ought to forget. They tried, in a few minutes, to give us a different perspective on the game. Then the coaches took over and analyzed the defense the Forty-Niners had been using against us, the play sequences we had been running, and the blocking we had been giving our ball carriers and the passer. They told us about the mistakes we had made and what we had to do to keep from repeating them. Then they went over to the other end of the room and gave the word to the defense —what was good, what was bad, what could be better.

There must have been just a little more than five minutes of the intermission left when they got both the offense and the defense together. We had only been together for a minute or so when one of the officials came in and told us that it was five minutes to kickoff time. That was our signal to head for the toilet, change any equipment that we wanted to change, and ask the clubhouse boy for whatever we wanted to eat or drink. I took a couple of oranges, as I always do. They seem to take care of my thirst and give me a little more energy, too. Shula talked to us in those last few minutes. He never really makes a speech, because he feels that it's very much each man's own individual problem to get himself "up" for the game, and I agree with him.

I think it's highly unlikely that anything the coach or anybody else might say could stimulate you to go out there and beat the pants off somebody. You have to want to do it yourself. It's everybody's personal problem. It's a game you're playing, sure, but it's also your living. If you're the kind of guy who has to be primed every week for every game, you aren't going to stay in the league very long. Shula just tells us how we've been playing, good or bad. He doesn't pull any punches. He's honest and he's fair, and that's all I think anybody can ask of a coach.

The one thing Shula was worried about this day was that, after winning six games in a row to come back real strong from a 34–24 beating by the Vikings on opening day, we might be getting a little cocky. Complacent is the word they use for it in the newspapers. Everybody who plays ball for a living knows

74

that as soon as you begin thinking you have it made, somebody is going to sneak up on you and clobber you. Shula didn't want that to happen to us—and neither did we. I don't think any of us were counting any chickens when we went back out on the field.

We received the kickoff and moved the ball for a while, then stopped. I was having a strange kind of a day passing. I thought I was throwing the ball on target most of the time, although I overthrew a couple of our guys badly—no excuse at all—but a lot of passes that looked like sure things were missing.

Jimmy Orr told me after the game, "You know, we dropped an awful lot of them out there today. I thought this was your best day of the year throwing the ball. I don't think anybody could throw any better. But we didn't complete too many, did we?"

We didn't. Fourteen out of twenty-nine, to be exact, and that's not what the sportswriters would call a scintillating performance. That first drive of the second half was one that should have gone all the way, but didn't, because we couldn't hit with the key pass when we needed it. Shula sent in the kicking team and had Lou Michaels try for a field goal from the San Francisco thirty-eight, but it went wide.

Then the Forty-Niners took over and began to go to town. It looked for sure as though they were going in, but our defense, which was tremendous all year, really gave it the old college try and held for downs on the eleven-yard line. It was a sight to see those two old men of ours, Gino Marchetti and Bill Pellington, tough old pros, ripping and tearing into the pileups and then, when they had held on fourth down and had taken the ball away from the Forty-Niners, running off the field jumping up and down with joy, more like a couple of sophomores than two thirty-eight-year-old warhorses with a combined total of twenty-five seasons in the National Football League behind them.

The third quarter ended without either team scoring, and for a few bad minutes I wondered if we were in for another of those patented Colt days when we roll up points without any sweat at all in the first half and then can't buy one in the second half. It's happened to us more times than I can count.

But it didn't happen this time. We lost a forty-four-yard touchdown pass to Jimmy Orr early in the last quarter and then missed another field goal try, this one from the thirty-seven. I felt sorry for Lou Michaels. He had piled up his car against a telephone pole at two o'clock in the morning a few days before, and I knew that at least half of the 60,000 people in the stands would be blaming the bad kicks on the accident and the broken curfew. The best way for us to take the heat off him was to do some more scoring, but the Forty-Niners got to it before we did. Our defensive line, which hadn't been scored on since the Packers game two weeks before, tried as hard as they could to make this one their third shutout of the season, but they couldn't quite do it. They held like tigers on the ground, but John Brodie, a good quarterback and a good passer, stabbed our secondary with enough passes to get the ball over. The last one was a two-yard job to Dave Parks.

That made it 23–7, and it might have meant trouble for us, because we had to give up the ball on a punt with nine minutes still left in the game. But the Forty-Niners got a bad break when Abe Woodson fumbled Kermit Alexander's lateral on the runback and Lou Kirouac grabbed the ball for us and took it down to the San Francisco nineteen. It took us four plays to get the ball over, but Lenny Moore finally made it with a leg-driving charge behind a great block by Alex Sandusky, and we were home free. That was Lenny's second touchdown, his thirteenth of the season, and it was a joy to see him running again like the old Lenny Moore.

Lenny is one of the most valuable football players in the

league. He is as fast as a jackrabbit and just as hard to get your hands on. His hands are as good on the end of a pass as Raymond Berry's, and that's the highest praise there is. Now that he was healthy after four or five years of having injury piled on top of injury, he was acting like a kid again, rocketing into the line with everything he had, not just running past guys but running right at them and even over them. Once he ran right up the backs of a couple of Forty-Niner linemen and made another ten yards before they got hold of him. It's hard to say how much it meant to our ball club when Lenny came alive again the way he did during that big eleven-game winning streak we put together in 1964. The thing is, there were—it's really no great secret—some guys on the club who thought he could have tried harder to get back in the game those other years. They thought he might have been dogging it a little. So this way, with Lenny as healthy as ever and trying so hard that he was practically spilling blood every time he went into the line, we not only were in the position of having picked up an additional player who was one of the two or three most dangerous runners and pass receivers in the league, but we had also solved a nasty little problem of club morale.

We didn't really need another touchdown, but that's always when you get them. Ordell Braase shook George Mira loose from the ball on Mira's first pass play after he went in for Brodie, and Gino Marchetti recovered it for us on their twenty-three. Shula sent in Gary Cuozzo at quarterback, and Gary got the touchdown on two passes, the big one to Joe Don Looney in the end zone. We went into the locker room with a 37–7 win for our seventh straight, the first time any Colt team had ever won that many in a row.

After-the-game is a good feeling physically and mentally and every other way when you win. It can be a pretty bad hour or so when you lose, but when you win it's a real pleasure to take the armor off, soak under the shower, nurse a cold drink, and play the game over with the reporters and with each other. It's a time I never hurry. I'm usually one of the last ones out. Dorothy says it's because it takes me so long to comb my hair and make it beautiful, but she's only being funny. She knows I comb my crewcut with a towel. I like to take a little time to unwind, though, and I don't like to be quick with the reporters, who always have a lot of questions they want to ask about what went on out there. Shula always wants to talk to me, too, and sometimes Carroll Rosenbloom is there, and Don Kellett. It's never less than an hour before I get out the door and meet Dorothy in the hall. Usually the people we're going to have dinner with are waiting with her. They were this time, and after we stood around and talked for a little while with my brother Len, who had driven in from Pittsburgh for the game, starting out at six-thirty in the morning, and was going right back now, we headed for the restaurant.

Dorothy had made a reservation for us the night before at a nice place in the apartment building at 3900 North Charles Street, and we were going to drive there—it's only about ten minutes from the stadium—in three cars. There were ten of us altogether. I always park my car right at the top of the ramp that starts up to the parking lot from the exit nearest the locker room, the way all the football players do, and there are always a bunch of people standing around there waiting for autographs and waiting just to talk to us as we come out. They're mostly kids, and women. Not girls, either. Women. They all know us well by now, and our wives, too, and we have a big conversation about the ball game before we go up the ramp to the car. This night (it's always pitch dark by the time we get outside) John Steadman of the *News-American* was standing out there blowing a toy trumpet that somebody on the Forty-Niners had given him because he had written a couple of pieces defending the right of their fans to blow those trumpet-charge calls at San Francisco home games even if it did blast the eardrums of some of their neighbors. We told him it sounded terrible, and he said we should have heard him before he learned how to play it. Then we got into our cars, the ten of us, and drove to the restaurant.

They were ready for us, even down to matchbooks on everybody's plate with "Welcome Unitas Party" printed on them. But that wasn't because I'm anybody special; they do it for everybody. Most of the others ordered a drink of some kind, and I had a bottle of National Bohemian, the beer that sponsors the Colt games on radio and television. I also worked my way through a bowl of vegetable soup, two thick double broiled lamb chops with a baked potato and an assortment of vegetables served family style—and another bottle of beer to help it along.

The manager insisted on sending two bottles of Piper Heidseick over to the table, to celebrate the victory, and it turned out to be quite a party. Dorothy kept us in stitches telling us about a touch football game the *News-American* had got two teams of Colt wives to put on for a special feature in the paper. "I said to them when they first asked me about it, 'Gee, why don't you just take pictures of us sitting in the stands and rooting,'" Dorothy said, "and I wish I had stuck to it. You should have seen us out there. It was a slaughter for both sides. They had me playing quarterback for my team and I went back to pass once and Flo Marchetti grabbed me and hung onto me like she thought I was Gino. I tried to get away from her and she grabbed my skirt and I could feel it beginning to come off and I said to her, 'Flo, this thing has gone far enough.' Believe me, if it had gone any farther—the skirt, I mean—we would have had to make those photographers burn up their films."

We talked about some of the things that had happened in the

game. There had been one freak play in the second quarter that gave us an easy touchdown, the fumble by Brodie that wasn't really a fumble because Brodie never had his hands on the ball. Nobody sitting around the table had known for sure what had happened. All anybody had been able to see, including me, standing on the sideline with Shula, was that one second Brodie was up over the ball on his own eight-yard line and the next thing we knew the ball was sailing high up in the air, and then there was a wild scramble and Steve Stonebreaker jumped up and snatched it out of the air and was running over the goal line with it. The reporters told us after the game that the way Brodie explained it to them, he had called a play to go on a quick count and had committed himself to the move and was in motion before the center snapped the ball, too late. The ball just sailed up in the air over everybody's heads. I guess you would have to call it a fumble, but it was the craziest fumble I ever saw.

Somebody wanted to know who had been awarded the "game ball," which is a tradition with our club, and I said it was Raymond Berry because not only had Raymond made some fantastic catches out there but the five catches he had for the day gave him 493 for his career and put him five ahead of Don Hutson, the old Green Bay Packer immortal. That left Raymond needing only eleven more to pass Bill Howton, a more recent Packer star, as the NFL's all-time champion pass receiver. A pass receiver doesn't beat out a Don Hutson record every day, and we thought Raymond ought to have the ball to remember the occasion.

The game ball can be any football, but it is supposed to be one that actually was used in the game. It goes to the player we think is most deserving after every game we win. For years, on our club, it was Gino who took charge of it. He would ask me and Alex Hawkins, as the other two captains, who we thought ought to get the ball. Then he would ask some of the linemen,

80

maybe Pellington or Raymond or Alex Sandusky. Generally, almost everybody agreed on the same man. It usually was obvious who had earned the football. Gino would give it to him, and later in the week the winner would bring it into the clubhouse and we would all sign it before practice, and it made a nice souvenir.

I won a game ball once, in 1956, when we beat the Rams, 56–21.

We talked about Mira's hard luck in losing the ball the first time he went back to pass, and about how mad Lenny Lyles was when the officials called him for pass interference on Dave Parks just before the Forty-Niners got their touchdown. I repeated what Lenny, who played with me at Louisville, had said in the locker room. "I don't complain if there's a shadow of a doubt that I might have fouled the guy," Lenny told us. "But how could I have interfered with Parks on that one? I was between him and the ball and I was looking at the ball all the time. I didn't even know where he was."

One of the men at the table wondered if I thought the officiating in the league was good, bad or indifferent, and I said I thought it was pretty good. The only thing that ever bothers me is every now and then when you run across one of those television hams who wants to steal the scene from the ballplayers. They over-officiate because they want to be on camera all the time. That can be a real pain in the neck, but fortunately it doesn't happen very often. I think the officiating has been getting better in the last few years since they've been bringing in some younger men, including some former professional players, who can keep up with the ball game better. I don't see how some of those sixty-year-old men can run up and down the field as well as they do. I admire them. But I think it's a good thing to get some younger men in there. Somebody said that even that isn't going to put a stop to the inevitable squawks on pass interference calls, and I agreed.

There is no question that this is the toughest call the officials have to make. It's strictly a judgment call, and five different men might give five different readings of the same play. You can bet your last dollar that the receiver and the defender won't agree on it, nor will the coaches or the fans of the opposing teams, which is why the officials can't possibly win when they make the call. It has to be a really flagrant case for the call to be made without a whole lot of complaining and arguing back and forth. What makes it so tough is that a lot of rough stuff that makes the fans holler for an interference call is really legal. If both men are going up for the ball, the defensive man can bang against the receiver pretty hard, can bump him right out of the way and maybe even actually knock him down, without being called for interference. But any deliberate use of the body or hands or legs in order to move the receiver away from the ball has got to be interference.

Every once in a while somebody came up to the table and asked for an autograph, and a few times the manager came over with menus or pieces of paper that people had asked him to bring over to me, but we were pretty much left alone to enjoy our dinner. For one thing, it's not a restaurant to which many people bring children. And for another, the atmosphere is quiet and dignified, or at least it was except for us. I don't think anybody who knows us would call Dorothy and me the dignified type. We had a good time, anyway. There is a waiter in this restaurant named Hugh, but Dorothy calls him Hush, and she and Hush put on quite a show. It was nothing, though, compared with the time we were eating somewhere else in Baltimore and one of the waitresses insisted on climbing up on top of the table so she could get a good picture of us.

It was a little before midnight when we drank the last of our coffee and started for home, back out the Beltway to Lutherville. It was about a quarter after twelve when I took our babysitter down the street to her house, and it was probably about twenty minutes after twelve when I fell sound asleep while Dorothy was saying something about what a pretty dress Mary Sandusky had worn to the game.

CHAPTER FIVE

A LEX HAWKINS is the captain of our special teams—the kickoff team, the punt team, the kickoff-return team and the punt-return team. Whitey is a fighter all the way, and I like him because he says what he thinks. Knowing him the way I do, I got a kick out of it when he told a reporter before the 1964 season started, "When the Colts win, it's a team victory. When we lose, it's Unitas' fault."

I'm not so sure that's the right way to put it, but there is no denying that for any pro football team to go well, the quarterback has got to go well. But the quarterback can't do it alone, either. You've got to have a balanced ball club, by which I mean not only a strong defense to go with a strong offense but also, just taking the offense, a good running game to go with a good passing game.

Back in the years when we were winning everything in sight, we had one of the best fullbacks the National Football League has ever seen—Alan Ameche. The Horse could bull his way through anything, and he was a wicked blocker, too. He could get the job done. We also had Lenny Moore, fresh out of Penn State and running like the second coming of Red Grange, and we had L. G. Dupre for good measure. The defense couldn't rush me too much, because if they did I would give the ball to Ameche, Moore or Dupre and our blockers would go to work and there would be dead bodies all over the field. We just didn't have enough running strength in the early 1960's, and inevitably that hurt us in the air, too, by making it easier for the defense to concentrate on breaking up our passes.

For a while, I remember, some of the writers and fans blamed our offensive line. They thought that with men like Art Spinney, Royce Womble and Buzz Nutter gone, we just didn't have it up front any more. But that wasn't the case. What we didn't have was a ground game. There is no such thing as a secret in this league, and it didn't take any time at all for the word to get around that all you had to do to stop the Colts was to keep Unitas from throwing the ball. I began to spend more and more time on the ground. I ate so much football between two o'clock and half past four on Sunday afternoon that I wasn't hungry Sunday night.

It wasn't until Jerry Hill took over at fullback and Tom Matte at halfback in 1963 that we began to come up with a running game that could scare anybody this side of Memorial High School. Then we really struck it rich in 1964 when we got Tony Lorick from Arizona State. Tony was our second draft choice for 1964, and the club never made a better pick. He's big, six-one and 215, and he can fly. What makes him something really special is that, like Moore, he combines his speed with a leg drive that gives him a wonderful second effort and helps him get away for another ten or fifteen yards, or even break away entirely, when you think you've got him stopped cold. The pickup of Joe Don Looney from the Giants gave us another running threat and another good pass receiver, and meant that the defense had to stay honest at all times. I might throw the ball to Berry, Moore, Orr, Mackey or Lorick. But I also might give it to Moore, Lorick, Matte, Hill or Looney and ask them to take it there on the ground.

Statistics don't always tell the whole truth, but you can bet on it that the big difference for us in 1964 was that for the first time in years we divided our gaining pretty evenly between running and passing. All you have to do is look at 1958, when our ball carriers picked up 46.9 percent of our total yardage and we won the championship, to see how important it is to have a balanced offense. Or look at the years when we didn't win anything, and notice that we went as low as 30.4 percent of our yardage gained rushing. In 1964 I was throwing less and getting more out of it because we were getting much of the job done by running the ball, and there wasn't a linebacker in the league who could guess what we were going to do on the next play. When I did throw the ball, I had time to do it right.

A good example of the way we were able to play it all that season was the second Green Bay game, which we squeaked through, 24–21. I completed only fourteen passes for 129 yards, and we matched those yards exactly with 129 racked up by our running backs. We never would have got the nine first downs we made passing if we hadn't made five others rushing. The Packers had laid for me in a big way when they were beating us twice a year in 1962 and 1963, but they couldn't do it any more. They had to worry about Moore and Lorick at least as much as about me.

We got our first touchdown on a drive from our own thirty-four. I hit Raymond a few times—not with anything long, though—and Lorick helped out with three or four good runs. The Packers stopped us on the eight and Shula decided to go for the field goal. Lou Michaels made it, from fifteen yards out, but the Packers were offside on the play. That meant, if we took the penalty, we would have the ball just inside the five-yard line, fourth down and half a yard to go. Shula made up his mind to go for it and sent me back in. I gave the ball to Lorick, the middle of our line opened up a great big hole, and Lorick shot through it for the touchdown. Michaels made the kick and we had a 7–0 lead. The Packers went ahead with two touchdowns in the second quarter, but we got back on the board with a field goal early in the third quarter, and then Moore put us ahead with a twenty-one-yard touchdown run.

A great goal-line stand that started with the Packers on our two-yard line, first down and goal to go, and ended with Paul Hornung missing a fourth-down field goal from the seventeen, saved our bacon for a while, but the Packers took the lead again in the fourth quarter when Elijah Pitts ran back one of our punts sixty-five yards into the end zone. We were in bad shape, losing, 21–17, and not much time left.

We got a break when Billy Ray Smith blocked a Hornung field-goal attempt on our forty and Jerry Logan picked up the ball and ran it down to the Green Bay twenty. If they had had reason to think that the only way we could move the ball was to pass, they would have blitzed me to death in that situation. But they didn't dare try it. They had to hold back. So I threw to Jimmy Orr at the five, where the referee called interference against them, and then I called Moore's signal. Lenny must have made up his mind that he was going to go over no matter what. He hit that line with everything he had. If there was any hole there at all it wasn't big enough to notice, but Lenny wasn't about to go down. He twisted and drove and lunged those five yards, and we had the ball game, one of the best wins we had had in years.

I heard Jerry Hill say in the locker room, "I feel like I just had a heart attack." That's the kind of a game it was. I can imagine how the Packers felt.

Probably the best illustration of what it means to have good balance in your offense is the series of thirteen plays that won

us the "sudden death" game with the Giants for the championship in 1958. That was our first playoff game, and we wanted
it badly. The Giants had won the championship four times and
knew what it felt like, but we were anxious to find out. But
the best we could do at the end of the regulation playing time
was a 17–17 tie, and Steve Myhra had to kick a field goal with
only seven seconds left to get us that, after Raymond Berry
had taken us seventy-three yards with three fine catches. It
didn't look good for us when the Giants won the toss before
the overtime and naturally elected to receive. Possession means
everything in a sudden-death situation, and the Giant fans
must have figured they had it in the bag.

But the bag had a hole in it. Myhra kicked off for us, a good
kick, and Don Maynard, who had a hard time finding the
handle at first, hung on to it and took it out to the twenty.
Frank Gifford made four yards off tackle, Charlie Conerly
tried to hit Bob Schnelker with a pass but missed, then Conerly
rolled out to his right and found himself without anybody to
throw the ball to. He ran for his life and almost got the first
down, but they don't pay off on almost. They had no choice
but to kick, and Don Chandler chased our safety man, Carl
Taseff, back to the sixteen to field the ball. Carl was hit hard
on the twenty, and that's where we set up shop.

A play that had been going well for us all day was L. G.
Dupre, our tight halfback, on an end sweep. We had been
making steady yardage with it, and anytime a quarterback has
something going real good like that, he likes to stay with it
until the other team begins to stop it. Generally, if they do
figure out a way to stop it, it means that they've changed their
defense one way or another to do it, and that ought to mean
that they've left themselves less protected somewhere else, and
it's up to you to find out where. Dupre got ten yards and a first
down for us, and we were under way.

I thought Lindon Crow had been playing Moore pretty tight,

so I slipped the question to Lenny if he thought he could get behind him. He said, "Well, it's worth a chance." I decided that since it was only first down, it was certainly worth a try, and as long as I threw the ball long enough and to Lenny's outside, there wasn't much chance that Crow would be able to intercept it. With two more downs to get the first down, I thought it was a good gamble. So I threw a big bomb to Lenny way downfield. We almost got away with it, but not quite. Crow just barely got his fingers on the ball and deflected it away from Lenny.

So it was second and ten, normally a passing situation, but I thought we could possibly cross them up by going with a run. We had been doing fine going wide with Dupre, and most of all I wanted to keep control of the ball. So I called a play where I faked to Ameche going up the middle and gave the ball to Dupre going wide. It worked for three yards.

That made it third and seven, on our own thirty-three, and this was where we could lose the ball. You either make the first down on this play or you have to pop. The third-down situation is probably the toughest call the quarterback has to make. Third down and long yardage is a hard call. You've got to know how the defense will be playing, and you've got to be able to rely on your own personnel to give you enough time to throw. This is one of the times when you have to pull out some of the information you've been picking up during the ball game and storing in the back of your head. What I thought here was that we had been hitting Raymond Berry quite a bit on short stuff, and we probably could keep on doing it. So when I went back with the ball, I looked for Raymond.

But the linebacker on the outside, Harland Svare, who became the coach of the Rams later on, was worried about the way we had been throwing to Raymond and dropped back to help the defender in the back, the secondary man. But he went back so far that he wasn't able to cover our fullback on a flare to the wide side of the field, the weak side, so I looked at Raymond and threw to Ameche, who just picked up the seven yards we needed for the first down. The linebacker, by not staying at home and by going back instead to help on Raymond, gave us a chance to pick up the first down. They were sure we would pass, and they were as ready as they could get, but they thought I would pass long. When I threw short to Ameche—actually, the ball only went about three yards in the air—they were hung up.

Jimmy Mutscheller had been doing a good job blocking Jim Katcavage, the Giants' left end, all afternoon, and of course L.G. had been running the ball real well for us, so I sent him on a sweep around our right end. It got us seven yards. That made it second down and three, and I figured it was time to throw again. I went back with the ball and looked first for Raymond and next for Mutscheller, and while I was looking a couple of guys hit me and we had a twelve-yard loss. You win some and you lose some.

I thought about throwing the ball away that time but I decided against it. That's how you throw interceptions. I would a lot rather take the twelve-yard loss and maybe come back on the next play and go sixty-five yards for a touchdown than take a chance on losing the ball. To tell you the truth, I didn't even have much time to think about it on this particular play, because Dick Modzelewski was back there staring me in the eye almost as soon as I raised my arm to throw. He had me cold.

So it was third and fifteen. I called a pass to Moore, but they double-teamed him in what was more or less a zone. They were so busy watching Lenny that I had plenty of time to go back with the ball and look for an alternate receiver. Carl Karilivacz was on Raymond, and he was sticking to him like glue, but then he slipped and fell for a second, and I tried to wave Raymond to go on further. But Raymond didn't know

Karilivacz had stumbled, and he just stayed pretty much as he was, which was good enough for a first down, so I threw the ball to him and he caught it for a first down on the Giants' forty-two.

Sam Huff, the Giants' middle linebacker, had been trying to help his secondary defend against our short passes. I had been noticing that he was dropping back a little more and a little more, and when I went back to pass again, I saw that he was a good four or five yards out of position. I checked off and switched to a trap play, up the middle with Ameche. I had two reasons for the play I picked. First, Modzelewski had just caught me real good and figured to be trying hard to get me again, which would make him fairly easy to trap. Second, Sam Huff, playing deeper than normal, would be an easy block for our off tackle, our strong side tackle, who would have to go through on this play and pick him up. The trap play hits quickly, and all we needed was a good trap on Modzelewski and just a shield on Huff as Ameche went up the middle. Everything worked just right. Sam stayed back and Modzelewski came in hard. Art Spinney trapped him beautifully and Buzz Nutter put the cat block on Spinney's man, Roosevelt Grier. George Preas, one of our good tackles, went down and put the big block on Huff, and Ameche shot through for twenty-three yards.

We were in good shape now, first and ten on their thirty-four. I tried Dupre again around the right end, but they stopped him for no gain. At least, though, we had Huff playing in tight again, and their left linebacker pressing in and worrying about a pass to the flare back, the one we hit Ameche with on the fourth play of the drive. Karilivacz was playing just a little bit deeper than usual, and I thought we would have enough of an opening to slant Raymond in quickly behind the linebacker and in front of Karilivacz. With the linebacker concentrating on covering the flare back, we should be able to hit Raymond with a real quick pass—a slant pass. We tried it, and it worked, and that put us down to the eight-yard line, first down and goal to go.

When you're in that close, you've got to try your big power play. We sent Ameche over right guard, strictly a power push, really an old-fashioned single-wing play, but the Giant line tightened up and we gained only a yard.

The next play was the big one, the one that everybody paid so much attention to after the game, mostly because they wondered why I took the risk of throwing the ball instead of running it and settling for an automatic field goal if we didn't make it. Well, in the first place, I've never noticed that field goals are all that automatic. They're a lot easier to block than punts are, and in a situation like this, where the Giants would be fighting for their lives against us, it would be no lead-pipe cinch to kick. And in the second place, or more likely in the first place, I didn't think the play I picked was so risky.

Actually, I called Ameche's signal again in the huddle. But when I came up to the line of scrimmage I was surprised to see that Cliff Livingston, their strong side linebacker, was playing inside of Jim Mutscheller. Normally a linebacker playing a tight end is going to play heads-up on him or a little to his outside shoulder. Linebackers are taught never to let the tight end release to their inside. So they generally play heads-up on him or maybe with their inside shoulder so they can force him to the outside. When I saw that Livingston was playing inside of Jimmy, I looked quickly at their left safety man, Emlyn Tunnell, and he was also inside of Mutscheller. I called a checkoff to a pass play we call a diagonal, where the end runs straight for the sideline. Their right safety man, Lindon Crow, was playing our flanker back, Lenny Moore, and I didn't think he could mess up the play, because he wouldn't dare leave Lenny and come in to try for an interception. If he did, I would have Lenny all alone in the end zone right now.

So we did it just the way I hoped we would. I took the ball back, checked Crow to see if he was staying with Lenny, saw that he was, turned and threw the ball to Jimmy so that it was going over his head toward the sideline. If he didn't catch it, it would go out of bounds. But he did catch it. He caught it and fell out of bounds with it a yard from the goal line. If he had fallen backward instead of sideways, he would have fallen into the end zone.

But we weren't complaining. We were only a yard away and we had two downs to make it in. Given that kind of a situation, and with a fullback like Ameche going for you, you don't do anything except give the ball to him, and that's what I did. Alan went banging off the right tackle for the touchdown with Nutter and Mutscheller making the big blocks and Moore going in fast and hard to throw a fine block on Livingston. The pictures of the game show that the hole Ameche went through was as big as the entrance to the George Washington Bridge. Nobody even touched him, and it was a great feeling watching him go over, I can tell you.

Our locker room after the game was a madhouse. It seemed to me as though the whole city of New York was trying to get in there. But it was a happy kind of confusion, and I didn't even mind the questions they kept asking me about why I went for the touchdown instead of the field goal and did it have anything to do with the fact that we were three-and-a-half-point favorites in the betting and anybody who bet on us would have lost if we had gone for the field goal, made it, and won by just three points. Nobody in an official position ever asked me why we didn't go for the field goal, and I never have thought they should have.

It's strictly a matter of judgment, and for that matter, it isn't even the quarterback's judgment. It's the coach's, because you go for a field goal only when the coach sends in the kicking team. As long as Weeb didn't do that, I kept going for the touchdown. The choice of plays, of course, was up to me, but I've explained that I didn't think the pass to Mutscheller was particularly risky, and all I can say is that if I had it all to do over again I would do it the same way.

One of the good things that happened to me in the locker room was that a man from *Sport* Magazine came up to me and told me that they had voted me the winner of their Chevy Corvette award as the most valuable player in the game. That sounded good to me. I wasn't sure what I, a married man with three kids, would be able to do with a fire-engine-red sports car with two bucket seats, but I was glad to have it. (I traded it in for a station wagon.)

The next couple of weeks were a big blur. I had had time to get used to being a professional football player whose name people had heard of, but this celebrity treatment was new to me, and even though a lot of it was pleasant, and anybody who says it isn't is just saying so because he thinks he ought to say so, it still takes some getting used to. It's like I was saying about eating out in restaurants: Some people are irritating but the great majority of them just want to be nice. I remember the day I came to New York to collect the Corvette on the Pat Boone Chevy Show. They were taking some publicity pictures of me with the car outside one of the Tudor City apartment houses on the East Side near the United Nations building. A boy who looked like he was about ten years old asked one of the photographers what was going on, and the photographer pointed me out and said, "We're taking some pictures of Johnny Unitas, the football player."

The kid cut out like a shot and ran into one of the apartments. He was back in a minute with a football, and he came up to me and asked me to autograph it for him. "I saw you play against the Giants," he told me. "My father took me. You were great." I signed the ball for him, but I couldn't help teasing him a little bit about it. "What's the use of my signing it?" I said. "It'll only come off as soon as you start playing with it."

"Oh, no, it won't," he said. "Nobody's going to play with this ball. I'll make my father get me another one."

We had a steak sandwich before the television show at a little restaurant near the studio, and Dorothy was all excited because Johnny Mathis was sitting at the next table. Then, after the show, we went to the Harwyn Club for dinner and the headwaiter showed us the corner table where Eddie Fisher and Liz Taylor had their celebrated rendezvous the night before Eddie flew home to Hollywood to tell Debbie Reynolds he wanted a divorce.

You know it was a long time ago.

CHAPTER SIX

T HEY TELL ME the total blitz, whatever that is, has doomed the drop-back passer, the "old-fashioned" passer who operates out of the pocket, the way I do. You're not going to play quarterback in this league anymore, they say, unless you are a scrambler who rolls out to pass and who runs with the ball not only when he has to flee for his life but whenever he sees a good opening. The quarterbacks of the future, I read in the newspapers, are all going to be like Fran Tarkenton, George Mira, Don Meredith and Gary Wood, not like Sonny Jurgensen, Bart Starr, Frank Ryan, Norman Snead—and Johnny Unitas.

You had better not believe it. It isn't true.

Whether you call it the red dog or the blitz, or even the safety blitz or the total blitz, the pass-rush will always be with us. The defense has got to go after the quarterback as fast as they can and as hard as they can. But they have to keep somebody back there in case the quarterback hands off to a runner or decides to throw and manages to get the ball away before anybody gets to him.

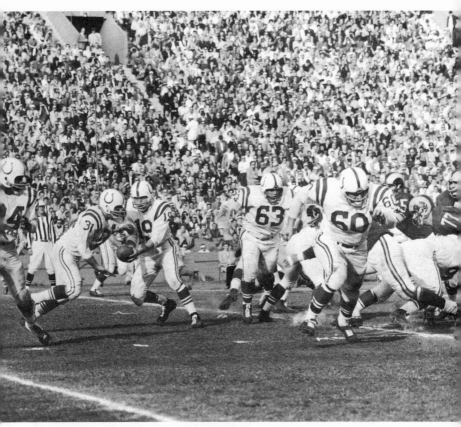

Our strong new running game wouldn't get very far if I didn't pay particular attention to the handoff. When we fumble on a handoff, I figure it's usually my fault. It's the quarterback's responsibility to put the ball where it belongs, with authority.

The big bomb has
always been an
important factor in
our offense, and
sometimes I will
throw a long one
even when our
chances of
completing it
don't look too good,
just to remind them
that I'm willing to
go deep. But the
bread-and-butter
passes are the short
ones that roll
up the first downs.

Nobody talks in the huddle except me. I will take all of the advice
I can get before the huddle forms, but once we're in it, I call the
plays. At that point, suggestions can only cause trouble.

You had better not take a job as a quarterback in the National Football League unless you are willing to be beat up a little. The men who play on the front four for every club in the league are monsters. When they hit you, you know it.

They call me an old-fashioned stand-up passer, as opposed to the scramblers like Fran Tarkenton and George Mira, but we all have to scramble sometimes. I'm no Lenny Moore, but you'd be surprised how quickly you can move when you're running for your life.

From the moment I first grip the ball as it comes back from the center, I'm ready to throw. I never change the grip after that first contact.

One of the biggest problems a quarterback has is keeping reasonably warm on the cold days in November and December. It can get pretty cold in Green Bay and Minneapolis. I don't like those chemical handwarmers, so I just keep huddled in my parka.

Nobody in the league can go faster or farther with a football than Lenny Moore. The fact that he's also a gifted pass receiver had a lot to do with his setting a new touchdown record in 1964.

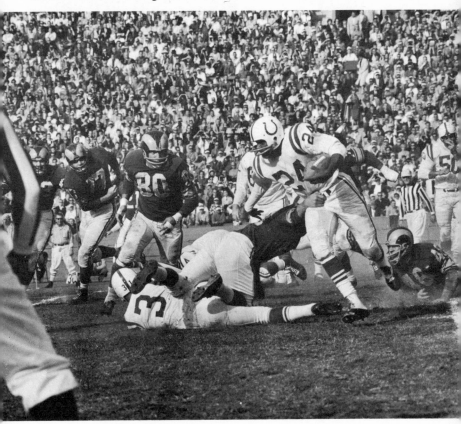

My favorite
receiver is, and
always will be,
Raymond Berry.
Number 82 has
more fancy moves
and stickier hands
than any other end
in the business.

I don't call as many automatics as I used to, but the checkoff is still important. If you can see that the defense is set up to smother the play you called in the huddle, it doesn't make any sense to stay with it. Fortunately, the coaches I've played for have left the decision strictly up to me.

I like to get dressed before the game early enough to allow some time for stretching out on the trainer's table and catching a nap. The hardest part about getting ready is yanking that tight jersey down over those bulky shoulder pads.

The President has the Secret Service to protect him, but I don't need anything like that. I have Jim Parker, Number 77, the best bodyguard any quarterback ever had. It's a comforting sight to see that massive body braced between me and disaster.

Neither Don Shula nor I look very happy in this picture and it probably isn't just because it was raining. The last few minutes of a losing ball game hurt.

What we're out there for is to put the ball in the end zone, and it's always a good feeling to see the referee's hands go up. They went up for us a lot of times in 1964—but not once in the playoff with Cleveland.

I don't think there is any noticeable difference in the amount of blitzing done in the league these days from the way it was in the 1950's. You will always have certain teams which, because of their personnel, are blitzing teams, and which will depend on the blitz as much as fifty percent of the time. You can be pretty sure these will be teams, like the Detroit Lions, that have three good linebackers who can make the blitz work and a secondary capable of covering pass receivers real tight. The heart of a successful blitz is a middle linebacker like Detroit's Joe Schmidt, who is probably the best in the business at calling the defensive signals. And Joe has two outside linebackers, Wayne Walker and Carl Brettschneider, who are tremendous blitzers.

Not every linebacker in the league is a good blitzer. Some of them are easy to block when they do blitz, and in their cases, so far as I can see, their teams would be better off if they didn't blitz. When you do it, you are taking one man or two men out of your coverage, and if the quarterback can spot it at the line of scrimmage, he can change the play and set up a one-on-one situation. That means the one defender has got to run all over the field with your pass receiver, and with his line backers blitzing, that one man is going to be in trouble back there. He can't make any mistakes, because if he does, and your man gets behind him, it's six points.

I would rather be up against a team that blitzes a lot rather than one that holds back more, concedes you an occasional short pass, and is in position to give you a lot of trouble when you go to the run or the deep pass. If you have planned carefully how to fight the blitz, what to do with your blockers and your receivers, you will probably get more good openings against a blitzing team than you will against a team with a looser defense. The biggest headache the blitzers give the quarterback is the way they obscure his vision. Those guys are so big that sometimes, even though you have time to get the ball away, and you have a man loose out there, it's impossible to see him through those enormous bodies in front of you. That's why, when the defensive front four come shooting in on us, we try to have our blockers shove two of them off to one side and two of them to the other side, at least a little bit, so I will have some daylight in the middle to look through.

You can fight any kind of a pass defense, including the blitz, better if you stay in the pocket and pay attention to all of the options you have as the play develops. Somebody asked me not long ago why I prefer to stay in the pocket, and I said because I don't want to get killed. I was kidding, of course, but I was more than half serious, too.

On just about any football team, even the Cleveland Browns with their great halfback Jimmy Brown, the quarterback is supposed to be the boss on the field. He is more or less your bread and butter. He is the one who throws the ball, and a whole lot of professional football is throwing the ball. He is the one who calls the plays and makes the necessary changes at the line of scrimmage. If he is going to be scrambling around back there in the backfield, running this way and that, twisting sideways and doubling back, he has got to be vulnerable to having the stuffing knocked out of him from the blind side—or any side at all. If he gets hit often enough, or gets hit in the right way, he is going to get himself hurt and be taken out of the ball game, and the team will have lost its number one man so far as moving the ball is concerned. That's not good sense and it isn't good football.

Just from the point of view of not wanting to take any great big losses, I won't go back over seven yards with the ball. I'll go back seven yards as the pocket sets up around me, and then move back up inside, or to one side or the other, depending on how I'm being rushed. With our blockers trying to move the defensive men to the outside, my best bet usually is to avoid the defensive ends by moving straight up in the pocket. If I can't get the ball away, and I'm taken down, I usually haven't lost too much yardage. Of course, when one of those monsters breaks through with the snap and is coming down on you like an armored tank as soon as you turn around with the ball, you've had it. Even so, the way I do it, the most I lose generally is seven yards. One of the "scramblers" might easily enough be dropped for twenty-seven.

Trying to look at it from the standpoint of the coach, I think if I were coaching and I had a quarterback who liked to run, and who could run, I would try to make up my mind once and for all how best to use him. I would have to decide whether my quarterback was primarily a runner or primarily a passer. If I decided he was a better runner than passer, I would set up a running-pass offense and rig my blocking accordingly. I would want the quarterback to be on the run as much as possible, with the threat of the running pass always there. But if I decided my man was primarily a passer, with the extra advantage of being not too bad a runner, I would make a pocket passer out of him. We would be better off, because then he would have time to survey the whole field before throwing, and when you're running all over the place, you can't do that. In order to see all of your possible receivers you have to be looking straight out in front of you. Also, it's much harder to throw on the run and be letter-perfect all the time.

There are a lot of good quarterbacks in the National Football League. Even the signing of Joe Namath and John Huarte by the New York Jets hasn't changed the fact that one of the major differences between the two leagues is the contrast in the quality of the quarterbacks. I don't like to talk about football players I haven't played against, so I'll confine myself to those I have played against.

One of the best is Norman Snead of the Eagles. Except for the fact that Dorothy thinks he's the handsomest quarterback in the league, I've always thought very highly of him. I think maybe his only fault as a quarterback is that he's too deliberate, too definite. He doesn't make quick enough movements. But he throws the ball well and he is smart. I think he uses his men very effectively. When he has the job all by himself and doesn't have to share it with King Hill or anybody, he will probably be even better. It may help him develop more confidence.

I think Sonny Jurgensen of the Redskins, the man who was traded by the Eagles for Snead, is one of the best passers in the league. He is strictly a passer, and he works out of the pocket. He doesn't run much and he doesn't scramble much. He just likes to throw the football, and you can be pretty sure he is going to do it the majority of the time. He is a good long passer, one of the best the league has had.

It's hard for me to say so, after the way the Browns ran over us in the 1964 championship game, but I have never been especially impressed with Frank Ryan. I think he throws a fairly good short pass, but he tends to throw the ball too quickly, to give up on the play too soon, when his primary receivers are covered. The frequent interceptions he had in 1964 convinced me that he throws the ball up for grabs too many times. But he does throw the short pass well, and as he showed against us, he has spirit. He proved that again the day a reporter told him about the Jets signing Namath for something like $400,000, including various fringe benefits like a Lincoln Continental, and Frank said, "If he's worth $400,000, I'm worth a million."

The Cardinals, who have been coming on strong since 1963, have an excellent passer in Charley Johnson. Charley has all the equipment of a first-class passer. He is quick with his hands, he has good speed, and he throws accurately both short and long. I think all he needs to become as good as anybody is experience. He needs to get to know his personnel a little better, so he can get the most out of their abilities, and out of his own,

100

too. Charley is a good one and he ought to be around for a long time.

Another good thrower who has been in the league long enough to prove just how fine a passer he is is Ed Brown. First with the Bears, for eight seasons, and then with the Steelers, Ed has always been able to hit his receivers a pretty fair percentage of the time, and for a quarterback, that's what it's all about.

Billy Wade, who lost his first-string job on the Bears to Rudy Bukich in 1964, is a hard case to figure out. When Billy is good, he is very, very good, but when he is having a bad day, he can drive you crazy. A lack of consistency has always been his problem.

I've always liked Earl Morrall of the Lions, probably because every time he has played against us he has been a demon. He is tougher on us than on any club in the league. He's just killed us. I think his coaches have made a big mistake not giving him the job and telling him it's his as long as he can keep it. But they have never done that. They have always made him split the job with Milt Plum, and, of course, that hasn't done either Morrall or Plum any good. But I have always liked Morrall as a passer and I have a special respect for him because he is so combative. He will drive you right into the ground to make a yard. He is a good example, by the way, of a pocket passer who can run very well when he has to and who is as hard to bring down as a fullback.

Fran Tarkenton is one of the most exciting young quarterbacks to come along in years. The Vikings have built a fine football team in the short time since they were organized in 1961, and they are going to be one of the best teams in the West for a long time. One of the main reasons why is Tarkenton. I think he runs out of the pocket, away from his protection, an awful lot when he doesn't have to, but he is a natural thrower. Anyway, he is the kind of quarterback who is at his best passing on the run. I think if you tried to keep him in the pocket he would have problems. He is the type who has to be allowed to get back there and jump around and dodge and reverse his field or whatever seems like the right thing to do at the time, and he does a tremendous job of it.

I still don't back away from my own conviction that this isn't the best way to do it, that you are asking for trouble running around back there like that. I wouldn't be surprised if Fran gets cold-cocked some day when he's trying to escape from one man and somebody else he isn't paying any attention to draws a bead on him. What it comes down to is that I've always been convinced there is only one way to run, and that is straight ahead. The shortest distance between two points is still a straight line. You are going to gain more ground by going straight ahead than you will by going laterally. You can pick up your receivers better if you set up looking straight down the field, and if you are really hung up, you can eat the ball with a minimum loss.

But what I think, and what I do, doesn't change the fact that Fran Tarkenton is a fine quarterback who has the makings of a great one, and a lot of people are going to get a lot of pleasure watching him do it his way. The name of the game is still touchdown, and if Fran can move the ball into the end zone, nobody is going to quarrel with the way he does it.

The Packers have probably the best short passer in the league in Bart Starr. I think Bart has a little trouble getting off the bomb, the deep pass, but I also think he plays it conservatively simply because that's the way his boss, Vince Lombardi, wants it played. Possibly he could do even better than he has if the coach would keep a looser rein on him, not control him so tightly. But you have got to do what the coach wants, and in this case the Packers have had a strong running team with Jim Taylor and Paul Hornung to carry the ball, and

Lombardi likes to combine his ground game with a short passing game.

This is a man who grew up in football as one of the Seven Blocks of Granite at Fordham, a great line on an old-fashioned powerhouse much like the Pittsburgh teams of Jock Sutherland with which Fordham played three straight scoreless ties in 1935, 1936 and 1937. Lombardi learned his football the safe, sure, grind-it-off-on-the-ground way, and that's the way he still likes it. The short pass is his concession to the way the game is played today, especially in the professional leagues, but he still regards the long pass as a dangerous toy that can explode in your hands and blow you to kingdom come. So Starr, who is one of the finest throwers in the game, throws less than he probably would on another team or under another coach. This is not to say Lombardi is wrong. The record says he knows what he is doing.

George Mira, who probably will end up with the job in San Francisco because John Brodie obviously isn't happy there and sooner or later they will trade him, was a scrambler in college, at Miami, and is still a scrambler in the pros. I think he's going to find out, one way or another, that he's going to have to stay in the pocket more than he is used to, and maybe more than he likes to, but there is no doubt that his greatest asset is always going to be a lot of play passing. He's quick, and he can run like the wind, and once he gets settled down, he is going to be good.

Our own backup quarterback, Gary Cuozzo, throws the ball, in my opinion, about as well as anybody. Of course, any quarterback—for that matter, any player, regardless of his position—needs to play in order to develop his skills, and Gary hasn't had much of a chance yet to show what he can do. It's a tough spot to be in, watching somebody else play all the time while you just sit there waiting for him to break a leg or something. But when Gary gets his chance, he will be up to the job. He can throw well, and he is a smart play caller. He has all the confidence in the world, and all he needs is a chance to work in with the team and have them get used to him.

One of the things that makes Gary's life frustrating is the fact that generally he gets to play only when we're well ahead and about all our coaches want to do is run the clock out. I can understand how he must feel after a week of throwing the ball in practice, to be told to go in there and just run the ball. He wants to throw. That's what he knows how to do. That's what he is practicing all the time. He wants to show the people what he can do. Every once in a while he just says the hell with it and does throw. He probably gets a few people mad at him when he does, but I don't blame him at all. In the first place, he has a mind of his own. Anyway, I think he's right. He isn't going to learn anything unless he gets out there and plays his own game.

A quarterback's greatest asset, aside from his own physical gifts, is knowing his personnel as well as he knows his own family. You have to know what every man can do and what he can't do. You have to know how long it will take him to run a move. Take a comparison between Jimmy Orr and Raymond Berry. You can call one move to Jimmy and call the same move to Raymond and it's altogether different, because Jimmy is quicker coming out of a move than Raymond is. Raymond is more deliberate in his movements, and he's more of a perfectionist than Jimmy. But Jimmy beats a defense on quickness alone. He can go deep in a hurry, and he's real fast going the long route downfield, so they have to play him differently. On the same play it would take Raymond a little longer to get there, so you would have a split second to do something else—to look away before you came back to Raymond. With Jimmy you can't look away too often. You can maybe take the time to "look off" Jimmy's defender by looking briefly at another receiver, but then you have to come right back to Jimmy.

I think Jimmy is going to be one of the great money players in the game. He is our clutch player right now, the man who is going to make the big catch for us. There is no better deep receiver around. Jimmy will catch one or two passes inside, and pretty soon his man will get worried and come in a little bit on him, and then Jimmy is gone. They will let Raymond catch passes inside longer than they will Jimmy because they're not afraid of Raymond going deep. Everything has to be perfect for Raymond to get out there for the bomb. He can't just beat his man straight down the field; he doesn't have that kind of speed. He has to rely on his bagful of tricks to get himself free, and by the time he does it, I have probably had to throw the ball. I can connect deep with Raymond only when my protection is really belting their front four and their linebackers on their tails.

Since Lenny Moore moved into the backfield in 1964, with so much success, I don't get many chances to throw long to him the way I used to. Coming out of the backfield, Lenny has a long way to go in order to get into position for a real bomb. It's easier to hit him with the short pass and rely on his speed to take it the rest of the way.

Usually, when you have a deep pass on, you like to have an alternate possibility built into the play. For example, in a 1964 game against the Rams in Baltimore, I wanted to hit Orr deep but I also wanted the alternative of picking up John Mackey short if that seemed better. I was sure, to begin with, that if we set up a flank-split situation, the Rams would rotate to a zone defense. So I went to the flank split and called our 62 zone pass. On this play, when Mackey rounds the linebacker, the safety man has to do one of two things. He either plays Mackey closely or he goes back to the corner. If he goes back to the corner, you hit Mackey as soon as he rounds the linebacker. If he hesitates a little, then stays with Mackey, Jimmy goes deep, trying to beat the halfback who has to cover the short outside area. The play calls for our fullback to go into that area, too, in an effort to overload it, and that means Jerry Hill will be forcing their halfback to choose between covering him or Orr.

The way it worked out this time, the safety man did play Mackey, and the halfback was worried just enough about Hill to give Orr the chance he needed to go all the way. I threw him the ball and he took it in for one of the three touchdowns he got that day. Jimmy is going to get a lot more touchdowns before he is through, and I hope I'm on the other end of all of them. I want Gary to have his chance, but not right away.

CHAPTER SEVEN

S
O FAR as the football player himself is concerned, the best thing that has happened to the game in a long time is the establishment of the other league, the American Football League. From a quality standpoint I don't think too much of the AFL yet. It seems to me they play strictly offensive football, and almost all passing at that. They have no defense at all. I know it has been said that some of their better clubs, like the Buffalo Bills or the San Diego Chargers or the Kansas City Chiefs, could beat some of our clubs. But I can't see it. I don't think they would stand a chance, principally because they don't have any defense. They aren't really complete football teams yet. But the fact remains that from a money angle, they have been great for the players.

Both leagues use a player draft, but it's a lot better to be drafted by two teams, one in each league, than it used to be, when you were drafted just by one team in one league—the only league. You didn't have much choice then. You either made a deal with the club that had drafted you and played for them, or you didn't make a deal with them and you didn't play for anybody. Now you can play one league off against the other, and you can come out of it making some important money. Everybody knows about all the cash that was showered on the top draft choices of 1964, especially Joe Namath of Alabama and John Huarte of Notre Dame, who are supposed to have taken Weeb Ewbank's New York Jets for $400,000 and $200,000, respectively.

I remember showing Dorothy a newspaper story about Namath signing. The headline said: "Ewbank Says $400,000 Quarterback Another Unitas."

"Yeah," she said, "only richer."

But Namath and Huarte weren't the only ones who got rich overnight. Craig Morton of California, who signed with the Dallas Cowboys of the NFL, and Dick Butkus, the Illinois linebacker who went with the Chicago Bears, are supposed to have been guaranteed $200,000 apiece. Fred Biletnikoff, the end from Florida State, went to the AFL's Oakland Raiders for $150,000. The grapevine says Tucker Frederickson, the Auburn fullback, got at least $100,000 from the New York Giants. It is interesting that the Giants claim they signed twelve draft choices at the end of the 1964 season for a total outlay of $400,000, or the price of one Namath.

Other players known to have signed unusually high rookie contracts at the same time were Larry Elkins, Baylor end, with Houston; Malcolm Walker, Rice linebacker, with Dallas; Jack Snow, Notre Dame's pass-catching end, with the Los Angeles Rams; Bob Hayes, the Florida A. & M. halfback and Olympic sprinter, with Dallas; Bob Timberlake, Michigan quarterback, with the Giants; Jerry Rhome, Tulsa quarterback, with Dallas; Gale Sayers, Kansas halfback, with the Bears; and Glen Ressler, offensive guard from Penn State, with the Colts.

But even though it's the money that has been handed out to the kids just graduating from college that gets all the newspaper publicity, the other league has been good for the older players, too. It's true that the large number of no-cut contracts may make it harder for some veterans to hold on to their jobs. But I think very few jobs will be lost that way, and most of those will be lost by men who couldn't have hung on very long anyway. And every club that throws around big bonuses and salaries to rookies is going to have to come through with money for the veterans. Furthermore, with two hungry leagues to be staffed, it's a lot easier for the ordinary player to keep going than it was before the AFL. And, of course, it's good for the player, no matter how old he is, or how young, who either doesn't make it or can't keep up the pace in the NFL. A whole string of former NFL players have made a good thing out of the AFL in its first four or five seasons—George Blanda, Tobin Rote, Babe Parilli, Ben Agajanian, Dick Christy, Len Dawson, and Jackie Kemp, for some.

I guess the only players who have been unhappy about the boom in bidding are the unlucky veterans who haven't been able to get their salaries raised in proportion to the new rookie scale. It's bound to annoy a veteran who has been doing a good job suddenly to find out that the club is paying more money to some untried rookie than they are paying him. I don't think it's fair to hold this against the club owners, though. It seems to me they are trying to do the best they can to compete in what has become very much a seller's market. The player who came in before the boom and who doesn't have enough bargaining power to get what he wants is unfortunately a victim of the times. All he can do is sit down and bargain with the man and talk up for what he thinks he ought to have. The chances are that if he is doing a good job for the ball club, they will pay him anything within reason to keep him doing it.

Actually, what is happening is that what most of the clubs are trying to do is keep everybody's base pay in line with the more or less established scale, but in order to sign some of the more desirable rookies they have to give out a lot of money in bonuses. Say you are paying a reliable five-year tackle $11,000 or $12,000, and this kid fresh out of college wants that much right now. If you want him that badly, but you want to keep his first-year contract down to $7,500 in salary, you have to make up the difference in his bonus. That way he gets the money and you can still tell your veterans that you are paying them more than you are the rookie, and supposedly everybody is happy.

One thing the pro football player has going for him that the baseball player doesn't have is the right, if he's convinced he's being treated unfairly, to elect to play out the option in his contract and become a free agent. The standard NFL contract gives the club an option on your services for a year after the expiration of the contract. But when the contract expires you can, if you wish, notify the club that you are going to play out your option, which means that you do not intend to sign a new contract with them but will honor the club's one-year option by playing one more season on the old contract.

The right to play out the option probably would be invoked by a lot more players these days, players who would want to leave our league in order to sign with the AFL for a lot of bonus money, except for the fact that if they do, they forfeit their NFL pension. Depending upon how long you have been playing, that can mean a pretty big sacrifice. You would have to get a great deal of money from the AFL club to make it worth while to give up your pension. Take my case, for instance. At the end of the 1964 season I had seven years of credit toward my pension (the first year that counted toward the pension was 1958), and if I chose to play out my option and then sign with an AFL club, I would be giving up a lot of money.

The basic pension for a five-year man, which is what you have to be in order to qualify, is $437 a month after you

110

reach 65. It's $656 for a ten-year man and $821 for a fifteen-year man. So it isn't likely that any player in my position would ever consider switching leagues unless somebody was going to put something like $250,000 in his hands right now. I wouldn't do it even then, as a matter of fact. I like money, but other things count, too. I have the feeling that I will be happier and my future will work out better if I stay with the Baltimore Colts and play the best football I can for them as long as I am able to. Assuming, of course, that they don't trade me away before I'm through, which can always happen in this game.

Some people have complained that it isn't fair for the league to deprive a player of his pension just because he goes over to the other league. Their argument is that if he earned it honestly it ought to be his to keep. But in fairness to the league I would have to say that I don't think it's particularly unusual in American business for a company to have a rule like that. I'm told that lots of pension and profit-sharing plans are operated with a similar penalty clause. It's the company's (in our case, the league's) hope that the pension will prove to be an added incentive to the employee to stay with the organization.

One thing I do think is wrong with our plan is that it is supervised by a board consisting of the commissioner of the league, Pete Rozelle, and two "independent" members appointed by the commissioner. The independent members are Edwin Etherington, president of the American Stock Exchange, and Clyde Vanderberg, a California public-relations executive. I think the players' association ought to have a representative, either an active or a retired player, on the board. It's only reasonable for us to want somebody there who would look at things from the player's viewpoint, somebody who would have a personal understanding of our problems. I'm sure that sooner or later we will get one. After all, the whole purpose of the pension plan, which is a good one, is to keep the players happy, so it only stands to reason that if the players want this one added protection that won't cost anybody anything, they are bound to get it.

We players are also working for an improved standard contract. It's perfectly understandable that the contract should be weighted in favor of the employer, the ball club, but we think it goes a little too far in that direction, and every year we try to get a few improvements in it. One thing we want is more money for the preseason games. The clubs make a lot of money out of them, but the players get virtually nothing. Up until 1960 we got exactly nothing. Now we get our $42 a week during the training season, which is better than nothing, but not much. We want it to go up to $100 as an in-between step, and then we will take it from there. Another thing we have to get changed is the amount of protection the player has when he is hurt in a preseason game or in training camp. Right now he doesn't have enough. With your contract going into effect only when the championship season begins, you are in a sort of Limbo during the training period.

I think without question a player who is hurt in practice or in a preseason game ought to have his contract paid in full for the year. But as it is, the club is required only to give him a chance to make the football team after he recovers, and I don't consider that very much protection. The biggest protection the player has, whether he's a rookie or a veteran, is that the club has to decide whether to hang on to its rights in him by putting him on the injured reserve list, in which case they have to pay him the salary called for in his contract, or cut him, in which case he becomes a free agent and can sell himself to the highest bidder. In the case of an experienced player who figures to have some good years left, that's enough protection, because the club isn't going to be eager to let him go. But in the case of a young player who hasn't had a chance yet to show what he can do in competition, or an older player who may not seem a good risk to come back after his injury, it's not enough.

Again, it's the new league that has been the biggest help to the player who finds himself in this situation. The NFL club isn't going to be too quick to let you go when the other league is waiting to pounce on you. But every football player would rather have his security written into the contract, because nobody knows better than he does how easy it is to get smacked the wrong way, or the right way, some Sunday afternoon and wind up not only unable to play another game of football but maybe even crippled for life. It stands to reason, anyway, that sooner or later the two leagues are going to get together the way the baseball leagues have, and then the players won't have the edge they have now.

One good result of their getting together will be a real World Series of football, which ought to mean a lot of extra money to the players, as well as a lot of additional pleasure for the fans. There still will be the money from the league playoffs between the two divisional champions, and with the money from the World Series, or World Championship, coming on top of that, it could put the football winners up on a par with the baseball winners, and I'm in favor of that. The television money from the game could be a boost for the pension plan, too.

The biggest problem I see in the idea of a World Championship game is the weather. The game would have to come late, even if the schedule isn't complicated by extra divisional playoffs within the leagues, and except when it happened to be in California or Texas, the weather would probably be terrible. I don't see how you could take care of it by starting the season any earlier than we do now, because practically everybody agrees that the baseball season runs right into the football season as it is. I know this sounds like a case of knowing which side my bread is buttered on, but I have always felt that baseball plays too many games. Of course, they say we could get more games into less time if we played twice a week instead of just once, but I don't think we could do it unless our teams added a whole lot more players, and I don't think the fans would like it if that happened. The football certainly wouldn't be as good. The plain truth is that it's tough enough playing one game a week with all that bruising physical contact. There are always a lot of injuries under the one-game-a-week system. Just taking quarterbacks alone, in 1964, Don Meredith, Roman Gabriel, Sonny Jurgensen, Y. A. Tittle and Bart Starr all missed playing time because of injuries. It would be much worse if there were less time between games in which to recover from the beating you took the week before.

So, if you can't start the season earlier because nobody wants to play or even watch football in hot weather and because early September naturally belongs to baseball, and if you can't schedule more games in the time you do have, the only answer is to play the World Championship in January. To me, that means you have to adopt a different plan from the one we use for the NFL championship game, where the site rotates from year to year, the Eastern Division champion having it one year (1964) and the Western Division champion having it the next year (1965). I think it would have to be agreed right from the beginning that the game would always be played in California or Texas and shown everywhere else on television. If we did it that way from the beginning, the way the Pro Bowl game has always been played in the Los Angeles Coliseum, I don't think people would object. I'm afraid they would kick up a big fuss if the NFL tried to adopt a plan like that for our present playoff game, because they are used to having it in their own city when it's their turn, and they wouldn't want to give it up. But I'm sure they would go along with something new that was set up on the basis of climate right from the start. They would understand that you can't schedule a championship football game in New York or Chicago in the middle of January.

Taking both leagues into consideration, the game could be played in any of six cities: San Diego, Oakland, Los Angeles, San Francisco, Dallas or Houston. It could be played in an American League city one year and in a National League city the next. Incidentally, if any Southern cities, like New Orleans or Atlanta, come into the leagues in the future, the game could be played in one of them.

I don't think, incidentally, despite the trouble the AFL had moving its All-Star game from New Orleans to Houston in January 1965, that the color question would be any problem. We play a fair number of preseason games in the South, and except for once a couple of years ago in Texas when they wouldn't let our colored players stay in the same hotel with the rest of us, which made us all feel bad and which has never been allowed to happen again, we haven't had any trouble. I doubt very much that any Southern city that would invite a pro football team to go there would expect to have segregated seating or anything like that, and aside from the fact that the new Civil Rights Act makes it illegal to refuse service to anybody in a public hotel, I think the Negro football players could be sure of being treated just as well in a city like Atlanta or New Orleans as they would be anywhere in the North.

Speaking as a player who may be around long enough to get into one of the first World Championship games, I hope the officials of the two leagues don't let themselves be talked into taking their chances on the January weather in the Eastern and Midwestern cities. I can just see all those fellows sitting around a conference table after a nice long lunch at 21 or Toots Shor's, telling each other, you know, it might not be so bad. Then, when it turns out to be eleven above zero, and snowing pretty good, on the day of the game, they would all leave their field boxes and go into the heated press box to watch the action. But we can't do that. We've got to stay out there and play football no matter how cold it is or how hard it is snowing.

Actually, you can get along fairly well even in bitter cold weather as long as the ground isn't frozen solid. But if it has been cold long enough for the ground to freeze, then you're in trouble. You can't get any footing. You can't run well, you can't get any drive into your blocks, and, of course, if you're a quarterback, it's murder to try and throw the ball. Sneakers can help the ball carriers a little bit, but nothing helps the passer much. I remember one time we played the Forty-Niners in Baltimore on a day when it was around twenty, and once when I went back to throw and cocked the ball the way I usually do, it fell right out of my hand. I had no feeling in my hand at all, and the ball just dropped to the ground.

Some quarterbacks use handwarmers, those little chemical things that look like cigarette lighters, but I've never bothered with them. I like to keep my hands in the pockets of my parka and keep them close to my body. The main thing is to keep moving. You can't afford to sit down or even just stand in one place. I keep doing little exercises with my feet to make sure they don't get too stiff and cold, because once that happens I'm no good for the rest of the day. It just kills me when my feet get really cold. I not only can't pass, I can't even think.

The other thing about playing on a frozen field is the way it feels when you get knocked down. It doesn't feel good. Let one of those 270- or 280-pound tackles nail you and slam you into that cement and it's just like running hard right into a brick wall. You can take a lot of punishment when you're playing on turf that has a little spring in it, but when you get hit on that frozen ground it doesn't give too much. You do all the giving. You can come out of a game played under those conditions looking as scratched and bruised as if somebody had worked you over with a set of brass knuckles.

116

Eddie Block has an idea that might solve the problem, although it wouldn't be cheap. He thinks somebody could manufacture a gigantic carpet, made out of some synthetic like Acrilan or nylon, that could be put down in big sections and cover the whole playing field. It would be sort of a sideline-to-sideline instead of a wall-to-wall carpet. "I don't see why the carpet people can't come up with a surface that would hold up under this kind of wear," Eddie says. "It will have to be tough, but I don't think that's too much of a problem. They have special cleat-resistant carpeting in some baseball and football clubhouses now, and lots of golf clubs have it, and it seems to work out very well." Eddie argues that a carpet like this would guarantee a uniform surface on the field, would absorb the shock of a fall even better than grass does, would never catch cleats the way turf does and therefore would save a lot of twisted ankles and knees, and above all would eliminate the problem of playing on frozen ground. I'm for that. I don't think Eddie is crazy at all; I think he's a genius.

So far as the prospects for even competition between the two leagues are concerned, I think it will take the AFL a long time to develop the kind of teams that could give the NFL a good fight. As things stand now, other than something like their best team catching our poorest team on an off day, I can't see them doing much against us. But I think that without a doubt they will improve. They have that big television contract to keep them going, and some of their clubs are beginning to draw very well. The Jets made New York a real two-team city as soon as they moved into Shea Stadium. There will be enough money to give them a chance to add some good new talent every year, and the teams are bound to get better as their men play together more and as the competition in their own league gets tougher. The biggest obstacle they will have to overcome in signing the better players coming out of college is the NFL pension plan, which is a big selling point and which the NFL owners use for all it's worth. But the AFL is bound to compete more effectively in this area before very long, and when they reach that point they will be on the way. The league is here to stay, I'm sure of that, and one of these days the World Series of football will happen. It can't come too soon for me.

CHAPTER EIGHT

W E'VE HAD OUR SHARE of outstanding football players on the Colts in the years I've been with the ball club, but I would have to single out two of them as the most amazing men I have known in my time in football.

One of them is dead. Big Daddy Lipscomb died long before his time and in a particularly sad and useless way. He made big headlines when he died, supposedly from an accidental overdose of drugs, in a second-floor apartment on North Brice Street, which is a kind of alley in Baltimore's "back of town."

The other one, Raymond Berry, is in my opinion the finest pass receiver in professional football. Raymond is a self-made star who is living proof of how much you can achieve by working at your job and thinking about it and struggling to improve your performance every minute of the day. It's an old joke that if there isn't anybody else around to throw a football to him, Raymond recruits his wife, Sally, to do the throwing, but it happens to be true. That's the way he feels about football.

Big Daddy, whose real name was Eugene, loved football, too,

and he was good at it. Part of the reason he was such a tremendous drawing card was his size, of course. He was awfully big. He was six feet, six inches tall, and he weighed about 285 when he was playing. I remember once when he was picking up some extra money wrestling in the off season he noticed that his weight had gone up to about 300 and he said, "I better knock it off a little. I don't want to look sloppy out there in my tights." And because he was so big, he was conspicuous. You could spot him real easy in every pileup, and he would do things the crowd liked such as bending down and picking you up bodily after he had knocked you six ways from Sunday, and he would say things like that famous line about "All I do is stop all those fellows coming at us and sort them out until I find the one with the ball."

But he wasn't just colorful. Daddy was a fine football player. One of the reasons I've never been able to believe that he used drugs is that as I understand it dope is supposed to dull everything for you, put you into a sort of a dreamy trance, and Daddy was probably the quickest man for his size I have ever seen, at least as far as lateral movement was concerned. With his quickness and his strength, and his incredible seven-foot arm spread, Daddy didn't let much of anybody get past him. "I won't say I'm the best," he used to say, "but on a good day I can't think of anybody who's better."

You can get an idea of how effective Daddy was from the fact that in 1958, our first championship year, he made more tackles than anybody else on the team, and that's a hard thing for a lineman to do, because in pro football most of the tackles are made by the linebackers. But Daddy just didn't let the ball carriers get through to where the linebackers could get at them.

He was a big kid personally, always clowning around and kidding. He was as quick to poke fun at himself as he was at anybody else, and everybody liked him. I don't believe he had an enemy on the ball club. I know people talked a lot about him and L. G. Dupre having a big fight in the locker room during the 1959 season, and Dupre was supposed to have missed a couple of games because Daddy stabbed him in the thigh. But that was all made up, the way most of those stories usually are. In the first place, if Daddy had ever got into a fight with anybody, he wouldn't have needed a knife. And in the second place, it never happened. How Dupre got to miss those games was that he woke up in the middle of the night with a big bulge in his thigh, a swelling that was as hard as a rock. The doctor said it was caused by internal bleeding, and they kept him out of the game for a few weeks. I think the fight story started after we traded Dupre to Dallas at the end of the season. It made a good "inside" story that we had had to get rid of Dupre because if we didn't he and Daddy would tear each other apart.

Daddy was always a favorite of the fans, and he capitalized on it by wrestling. He wasn't very good at it, but I guess you don't have to be as long as you have the kind of body Daddy had. He liked to ham it up, too, so he put on a pretty good show. We used to give him a hard time about learning his lines and remembering to lose when he was supposed to, and all that, but he took it good-naturedly. "People are always asking me about this 'fix' business," he told a reporter once, "but all I know is I just do the best I can and nobody has yet told me whether I should win or lose. I don't know about the other guys. I don't ask, either."

It's a fact that Daddy gave up the wrestling when some promoter wanted to change him from a good guy to a bad guy. He wouldn't do it. "That ain't Big Daddy," he told us in the locker room. I always thought he just couldn't see himself facing the kids if he had to be a villain in the wrestling ring, and he cared a lot about having the kids look up to him. He was crazy about kids.

Daddy never had much time to be a kid himself. He never even knew who his father was, and for the first eleven years of his life he lived with his mother in a furnished room in Detroit. Then, one night, a policeman came to the room and told him that his mother was dead. She had been standing at a bus stop, just waiting for a bus, when a man she knew came up and stabbed her forty-seven times. After that he lived with his grandfather, his mother's father, and he had to work to pay for his room and board. He was a dishwasher in a restaurant for a while, and later on he shoveled sand and gravel on a construction job. "There was a time," I remember him telling us, "when I worked the midnight-to-eight shift in a steel mill and then went home and put on a clean shirt and went to school."

Daddy never went to college. He played his first football at Miller High School in Detroit and then made his reputation playing for the Camp Pendleton Marines in California. The Rams drafted him in 1953, but he never made it big with them, and they put him on the waiver list in 1956. The Colts picked him up for the waiver price, $100, and with us he made All-Pro three times and helped us win a lot of football games. He was still a good tackle for the Steelers after we traded him there. Kellett let him go, I guess, because although he was supposed to have been born in 1931, nobody ever was really sure how old he was, including himself, and the club figured they had got what they could out of him and wanted to get something for him before it was too late.

It's hard to believe about a man as huge as he was, and as powerful as he was, but Daddy was always afraid to be alone, especially at night. "I been scared all my life," he said once. "You wouldn't think it to look at me, but I have been." The night he died was typical of the way he kept looking for somebody to be with all the time. From what I read in the newspapers, he was planning to drive to Pittsburgh the next morning to sign his contract for the 1963 season. According to Buddy Young, who knew him better than anybody, he was going to get

122

a two-year contract for $15,000 a year. He played in a softball game in the evening—it was early in May—and after the game he went partying with another fellow and two girls. They took the girls home in Daddy's yellow convertible at three o'clock in the morning, and then they drove down to what Baltimore calls the Block, which is where most of the late-night action is. The man who was with him says he bought $12 worth of heroin for them, and he says Daddy began to froth at the mouth after he took it and keeled over on the kitchen floor. They called the police and an ambulance came and took Daddy away, and he died in a few minutes.

I've never been convinced that Big Daddy took heroin willingly. For one thing, he was right-handed all the way, yet the needle marks were on his right arm. For another, he, like Jim Parker, hated needles like poison. We'd have to back him into a corner to get him to take a tetanus shot.

His funeral was something special. There must have been thousands of people there, including all three of Daddy's ex-wives. "I didn't mind losing her so much," he had said about one of his wives, "but I sure minded losing my 1956 Mercury to her. I loved that car. It was the best car I ever owned." Most of the cars at the funeral were Cadillacs. Daddy went out first-class.

The only thing Raymond Berry has in common with Big Daddy Lipscomb is that he also is a great football player. I don't expect to see a better pass receiver if I stay in the league another ten years. Raymond does it with only nine fingers, too. He doesn't get any use out of the little finger on his left hand, because he broke it in high school and dislocated it five times in his first season as a pro. But he does all right with the fingers that work. It doesn't even bother him that he has to wear extra-large contact lenses when he plays because he can't see a thing without them. He's as blind as a bat. He can't even see the big letters on the eye doctor's chart, much less the small ones. But he can see that football when you throw it to him, and he can catch it like nobody's business.

Raymond played college ball at Southern Methodist, where he was good but not remarkable. The Colts drafted him as their twentieth pick as a future in 1953, just barely giving him the nod. But when he showed up at training camp in the summer of 1955 he wasted no time convincing the coaches that there was more to him than met the eye. He wasn't very big, six feet two and only 184 pounds, almost fragile for an offensive end in the National Football League. His biggest claim to fame was that one of the news services had picked him at end on the All-American Academic team, and unhappily, being a good student isn't exactly the first requirement for winning a job in professional football. Nobody holds it against you that you're smart, but first you've got to prove to them that you can, as Casey Stengel says, execute.

Raymond made sure that everybody knew he was in camp. He went to bed at half past eight, to make sure he got enough sleep, and once he got a pair of uniform pants that fitted him just the way they should, he insisted on washing them himself so they wouldn't be given out to some other player after the laundry was done. He carried a football with him every place he walked around the camp grounds so he would get the feel of the ball and keep his fingers supple enough to catch any passes that might be thrown to him. It wasn't long before his name was a byword on the club for dedication and hard work, and that kind of a reputation never hurt anybody. Raymond survived all the cuts and played well every time they gave him a chance. By the 1957 season he was good enough to finish up with forty-seven catches for the second-highest total in the league, and in 1958 he tied Pete Retzlaff for the most receptions. He was the leader all by himself in 1960 with seventy-four receptions for 1,298 yards, and he was All-Pro in 1958, 1959 and

1960. He has caught more passes, 506, than any man in the history of the National Football League.

We used to use him only for short passes. He was our "saver," the guy we threw to when there was no chance to go deep, the man who would give you the sure gain. We don't restrict him that way any more, and every once in a while Raymond will catch a deep one. He never has been what you would call fast, but he makes up for it with the best collection of moves in the business. Raymond can fake you right out of your shoes. And when you throw the ball to him, he holds on to it like glue. Whenever anybody says, "Practice makes perfect," I think of Raymond, because it is practice that has made him what he is. He never stops. You have to drive him off the field at the end of the day, and then he goes home and, after dinner, gets Sally to throw a couple of dozen passes to him in the back yard. When he isn't actually catching a football, he is busy thinking up new fakes, plotting something that will be new and different to spring on the man he will be playing opposite in the next game.

Raymond even works on the airplane when we're playing on the road. One of our Baltimore football writers, Bob Maisel, sat behind Raymond and Gary Cuozzo on a flight to Detroit and was astonished at the way they went over plays and personnel all the time we were in the air. But that's Raymond for you. He doesn't stop working, or thinking, when the last practice is over. Sometimes he comes up to me in the locker room while we're getting dressed and pops a new idea he just got. It isn't that the other fellows don't think about the game a lot, too. It's just that Raymond never stops.

"As far as I'm concerned," he says, "you can play the game one of two different ways. One is what I call the grab-bag method, coming up to a certain situation and saying, 'Well, it's second and ten and we're on our own thirty, so it's time to run a slant pass.' If you do it that way you come up with ineffective plays and interceptions. The other way is to remove as much of the element of chance as possible before you even go out on the field. That's what we try to do. It's a long, slow way of doing it, but I just don't know of another way it can be done. You might think you have the best pass pattern in the world, but against a certain defense it isn't worth a thing. What we try to do is eliminate those plays that don't have a chance of working against the defense we know this particular team is going to use against us, and substitute others that might go well against that defense. Football is an uncertain game at best, but the more uncertainties you can get rid of before you start to play, the better chance you have of accomplishing what you set out to do on Sunday afternoon."

Amen.

CHAPTER NINE

"I BEEN RICH and I been poor," Joe Louis is supposed to have said once. "Rich is better." Any professional athlete knows what he means. I've been on winners and I've been on losers. Winners is better.

One of the nice things that happens to you when you have the kind of season we had in 1964 is that you find out that you and a lot of the fellows you play with are all-this and all-that. The award season in pro football begins the week before the last game of the year. That's when the Associated Press announces its All-NFL team, picked by three football writers from each city in the league. I was the all-league quarterback in 1957, 1958 and 1959, when our club was hot. In between, when other clubs like the Packers and the Giants were hot, other quarterbacks, like Bart Starr and Y. A. Tittle, were all-league. But in 1964, because Lenny Moore, Tony Lorick, Raymond Berry, Gino Marchetti, Bill Pellington, Jim Parker, Alex Sandusky, Bobby Boyd, George Preas and thirty other football players made us a winning team, I became the best quarterback in the league again.

There is a whole lot of nonsense about this "all" stuff. For instance, Ordell Braase of our club has never made all-league, not even the second team. Not because he hasn't deserved it—he has—but simply because there is an unwritten rule that no team gets more than one man on the squad at the same position, and we have Gino Marchetti at the other defensive end spot practically every year. For the same reason, Alex Sandusky didn't even make the second team until 1964. Jim Parker was always there, and they weren't about to put both of our offensive guards on the team. I can understand how people would come to feel that way, but that doesn't make it right. The plain truth is that, whether it's All-American or All-NFL or All-Anything, it's impossible for any committee to pick out the eleven or the twenty-two best players. Most of the time the men who are doing the voting haven't even seen all of the players. They vote on the strength of their publicity. So the winners collect the prizes, and the losers say, "Wait till next year."

We not only had Marchetti, Moore, Parker, Boyd and me on the All-NFL first team and Sandusky, Preas and Pellington on the second team, but we also picked up three other awards. They gave me the Most Valuable Player award, picked Don Shula as the Coach of the Year, and voted Lenny Moore as the Comeback Man of the Year. The only place we lost out was on Rookie of the Year, where Charley Taylor of the Redskins won over Tony Lorick.

It pays to win. In 1963, when we were looking bad against the Bears at Memorial Stadium, in the middle of what had been a real bad season up to that point, the fans were giving me a pretty good going-over. "We want Cuozzo!" they kept yelling. Shula stuck with me, and we won five of our last six games and finished third in the West. He stuck with me in 1964, and we

128

won the Western Division. All of a sudden I was all-league again, and nobody said anything about wanting Cuozzo.

But I meant what I said when they told me about the MVP award in the locker room after practice on the Thursday before our last game with the Redskins. "I appreciate the honor," I said, "but I've had better years. Bart Starr and Fran Tarkenton had outstanding seasons. They deserved something. I think we've got forty players on this team who should have been given the award. Football is still a team sport, and it takes a team to win."

Once you've got your division championship locked up, you start looking ahead to the playoff game. We began doing that in '64 after we clinched the West by beating the Rams, 24–7, on Sunday, November 22, in Los Angeles. That was our tenth straight, which wasn't half as important as the fact that it was the big one. After that we concentrated on staying sharp ourselves and rooting for the Browns to win in the East. We had to root for the Browns over the Cardinals because their stadium seats 80,000 compared with only 32,000 for Busch Stadium in St. Louis, where the Cardinals play, and that meant a difference of maybe $4,000 apiece in the winning players' shares and probably $2,500 or so in the losing players' shares. We were disappointed when the Cardinals beat the Browns, 28–19, in the next-to-last game, to stay alive, but when the Browns ran all over the Giants in their last game, to wrap it up, we were sure of the biggest gate in the history of the playoff.

In addition to worrying about the size of the stadium in which the championship game would be played, we had to worry about staying sharp. We looked bad losing to the Lions, 31–14, but we consoled ourselves with the excuse that we had been due for a bad game and it was a lot better to have it in a meaningless regular-season game with the division title already clinched than in the big one. This theory sounded even better after we jumped all over the Redskins, 45–17, in the last game. We were only so-so in the first half of that one, which ended in a 10–10 tie, but in the second half we played the best football we had shown in weeks. We came up with two touchdowns in the third quarter and three more in the fourth, and our defense racked up the Redskins like it was practice. Two of our boys took new National Football League records out of the game, Lenny Moore for the most touchdowns in a season, with twenty, and Raymond Berry for the most pass receptions in a career, with 506—a record he will be breaking every time he catches a pass as long as he stays in the league. All in all, we felt pretty satisfied. Last Sunday, we figured, had been just one of those days.

We had two weeks to get ready for the Browns. Shula gave us the first two days off, which gave us a chance to get our Christmas shopping done, and we didn't do much on Wednesday except loosen up for a little more than an hour, running some screen passes and draw plays, trying to work out the soreness and stiffness. On Thursday the coaches gave us the offensive game plan, and on Friday we got the defensive game plan.

I worked just as hard on one of our defensive practice days as I did on the offensive days. Gary Cuozzo and I took turns being Frank Ryan and running off Cleveland plays. Jerry Hill was Jimmy Brown, Raymond Berry was Paul Warfield, John Mackey was Gary Collins—everybody was somebody on the Browns. We did our best to run the plays just the way Cleveland did, so that when we were in the actual game our defense would know how the coaches wanted them to react to any given Cleveland offense or pass pattern. We would spend about half an hour on their pass offense, with Gary and me alternating throwing the ball and our secondary trying to knock them down or intercept them or in any way make them incomplete, and then we would go through their running offense, with all of our defensive team coming together against us. Basically our coaches tried to set up specific defenses for the offensive formations they felt sure the Browns would use, and the hope was that the more we ran those formations against them, the more accustomed our defense would get to handling them. We tried to give our defense a real good picture of what the Cleveland offense was going to throw at them.

A lot of our preparation consisted of looking at movies of Cleveland games. We had ten of their games, six of which we got from them and four from other clubs. I watched at least one Cleveland game every day the whole time we worked for the game. In addition to the ones I saw during the day at the stadium, I used to take one home almost every night and run it off on the projector in the family room. The movies help a lot in your planning. I've heard it said that the Cleveland coaches think they learned the secret of how to stop our running game by studying pictures of our two games with the Vikings, who beat us once and almost did it twice. The movies we get are pretty good. They are shot with two cameras, so that you have a sideline shot and an end-zone shot. Every once in a while you get a bad one. Two of the Cleveland films we had, the Steelers game and the Eagles game, weren't so good to work with because they were a little pale and blurry, but mostly the quality is pretty consistent. We ran those films, especially certain parts of them, over and over, looking for little things that might help us, and we thought we had found a few.

On Saturday, that first week, we spent all day going over the Browns' various red dogs, or blitzes, getting ready to take care of whatever blitz they might use against us in any given situation. The Browns have never had the reputation particularly of being a blitzing team, but you don't win a division championship in our league without putting on a strong pass rush, whether you call it a blitz or not, and we tried hard not to make the mistake of taking anything for granted. I remember being impressed by something Blanton Collier, their coach, said in an interview before the game. "You might say we don't blitz well," he said, "but I don't think you can say we don't rush much." Then he said, "Don't forget, if you blitz and don't get to the passer, you are worse off than if you didn't blitz at all." I should have paid more attention to him.

A lot of our work that Saturday was simply getting used to reacting to their blitzing so that I would be able to change whatever plays would have to be changed at the line of scrimmage to counter it. Most blitzes you can pretty well expect from a given team in a given situation, and you take that into consideration when you call the play in the huddle, but sometimes you see something when you go up over the ball and you know you're going to get killed if you don't check off. Mostly, though, it's a question of calculating what they are going to do on the basis of what they have done before.

Some things you just know without any doubt. Say it's second down and thirteen, and this is a team that likes to blitz, you know they are going to do it here. They are going to do everything they can to put you in an even worse situation than you are in. So if you can change a play, or if you can get a key on a man, you're going to do it to try to make their blitz less effective. A lot of times they will tip off the blitz by having the linebacker play in a little closer, and if you can pick this up from the movies, or at the line of scrimmage when you're about to call a play, you can change the play or at least change the assignments of some of your men and take advantage of something that otherwise would be very bad for you.

A lot of times defense will come up tight and try to make you change your play and then drop back in a recovery position and catch you. It's all a guessing game. As you study the films and study the scouting reports that you have on them, they generally fall into a sort of pattern. They generally like to blitz on a certain down. Or take a blitzing team like Detroit, if they get you in a hole, say down around your own fifteen-yard line, you can be pretty sure they are going to blitz you with everything they've got, on the theory that if they can just catch you once or twice more, you will really be in trouble. So that was what we did all day Saturday, work on covering those linebackers shooting through on blitzes. Sunday we were off, and Monday we were off.

On Sunday I just sat around the house after I came back from Mass. In the afternoon we watched the AFL football game on television. That was the Buffalo–Boston game, which Buffalo won, for the Eastern Division championship. I thought it was a pretty good game, although I can never understand how they let those pass receivers run around all by themselves out there all day. It's more like basketball than football.

Monday the team was off, there was no practice, but I was down in the office at the stadium watching Cleveland films.

Tuesday we were back at work, and every day that week we were out on the field for practice at twelve o'clock, taped and ready to go. We usually kept at it until three, each day working on some one particular thing. One day all we did was goal-line stuff, plays we would use inside the ten-yard line. Wednesday was another offensive day, with our defensive team setting up Cleveland's defenses against our plays. I had been impressed by what I had seen of Cleveland's young tackle, Jim Kanicki, in the movies, and, of course, we knew all about the other tackle, Dick Modzelewski, the old Giant, who had been one of the good players in the league for a long time. But I thought that our offensive guards, Parker and Sandusky, had played against even better tackles in the West, men like Alex Karras of the Lions, Merlin Olsen of the Rams, and Henry Jordan of the Packers, who are generally regarded as the best the league has at their position, and I frankly hoped that we would be able to contain their pass rush enough to get the job done. It was a good work-out that Wednesday, and I was encouraged.

From the standpoint of spirit, Thursday was even better. That was a defensive day, and the coaches decided it would be a good idea to have some real contact work, a good hard scrimmage, so they had us run Cleveland goal-line plays against our

133

defense, and they turned everybody loose to hit hard. Well, actually, the offense was only supposed to work at about two-thirds full power, but the defense was supposed to go all out. Maybe it was because the defense wasn't doing so well, or maybe it was just because when you're trying to hold back a little bit, you're much easier to knock down and stomp on, but anyway a few of the guys got sore at each other. It got a little bit rough. The defense, as I said, wasn't looking too good, so they probably decided they would show us up. Well, everybody on the line went right at it with hard blocking and tackling, and a couple of guys got hit real good. You might say there was a little altercation. Nothing serious, just everybody was banging everybody else for a while, and Joe Don Looney even took a punch at one of our tackles, John Diehl. Those things will happen. It's good, in a way. It shows that the guys are there and that they want to play.

We trimmed our Christmas tree that afternoon. A couple of our friends came over to the house to see us, and to bring presents for the kids, and they helped us put up the tree and get all the decorations out so the kids could trim it. I put the lights on, but they did all the rest of it, with Janice in charge and Johnny being the first sergeant, yelling at Chris and Bobby not to break anything.

Christmas morning, Friday, I got up at about seven o'clock. The kids were racing around our bedroom, trying to get us out of bed, insisting that they wanted to go right downstairs and see what was under the tree for them. So Dorothy and I gave in. The tree was in the family room, and with the kids tearing all that paper off those packages and shouting about each new present they opened, it was like a Chinese fire drill in there. I couldn't stay long, because I had to go to eight o'clock Mass in order to have time for breakfast before heading for the stadium. Shula had called practice for twelve o'clock, as

134

usual, which meant getting to the stadium by eleven to get taped and dressed.

A great big Santa Claus with a suspiciously dark face put on a funny show in the clubhouse before practice, doing a reindeer dance with a big bag of toys that turned out to be full of Fred Schubach's footballs. I was pretty sure it was big Jim Parker, and then, when he turned around and said to Lenny Lyles, "Hey, Leonard, I thought you said there wasn't no colored Santa Claus," I knew it was.

We weren't supposed to leave for Cleveland until Saturday morning, but there was some doubt on the part of the club and the league officials that it was going to be safe to wait. They were afraid the weather would turn bad and we might not be able to fly. They were talking about a couple of inches of snow, and fog, and all kinds of trouble. It sounded pretty bad. So they talked back and forth, and they talked to the man from United Airlines, and finally they decided to have us all come back to the stadium at eight o'clock Christmas night, take a bus out to the airport, and fly out then. We didn't get finished with practice until about three o'clock, so that didn't leave us much time at home.

But I don't think anybody minded. We were all ready for the game to be played, and we didn't want to spend all day Saturday sitting around the airport or landing in Montreal or Boston and then running for a train. I think it was Gino who said, "I'm just as happy to go out there on Christmas. We've come this far, and there's only one more thing to be done, so there's no sense letting anything interfere with it." We did have time for dinner at home, anyway.

After what happened to me next, I should have known what was going to happen to us in Cleveland. I looked at my watch a couple of times to make sure I was leaving enough time, and the last time I looked I had about half an hour before I thought

I ought to leave, which was seven-thirty. It takes me just about half an hour to drive comfortably from our house to the stadium. So I took my time saying goodbye to everybody, and getting my car out of the garage, and I remember looking once at my watch as I was starting down the Beltway and saying to myself that I had plenty of time. It was only a couple of minutes after seven-thirty then. When I pulled into the stadium parking lot, there were some ice skaters around, but no buses and nobody from the ball club. I looked at my watch again and it still said a few minutes after seven-thirty. No wonder everybody had gone. Obviously, my watch had stopped, and I didn't know when or for how long. I asked one of the ice skaters what time it was, and he said it was half past eight. I got back in my car and debated briefly whether or not I ought to take time to call the airport and tell them I was on my way. I decided against it because we had permission to drive ourselves if we wanted to, instead of taking the bus, and I knew they would simply assume that was what I was doing. Well, it was, but not because I wanted to.

As if things weren't bad enough, I noticed as I headed out North Charles Street that I had hardly any gas in the tank. But it was Christmas night, and as I drove along, I didn't see a gas station open anywhere, so I just kept on going, hoping I would make it. At least to that extent, I was lucky. It was close, but I did make it. What an omen, though.

We left Baltimore a few minutes after nine o'clock, and naturally, I lost almost every hand in the poker game in the back of the airplane. I should have turned around and gone back home right then. Instead, though, I checked into the Cleveland Sheraton with everybody else at about half past eleven, ate a couple of hamburgers with a cup of coffee, and went to bed.

I went to Mass at St. John's Cathedral in the morning with Shula and Alex Sandusky, then went up to my room for a while and studied my play book. Later in the day, at about one o'clock, we went to Cleveland Stadium for a short workout, just along the sideline because they had the field covered by a tarpaulin and a whole lot of blower-type heaters. When we walked out on one of the ramps to take our first look at the field, we were reassured by the sight of the heaters. It was encouraging to know we wouldn't have to play the game on a frozen field. The Cleveland officials deserve a lot of credit for the work they did and the money they spent to make sure the field was in good condition. They even set up a blower-heater at each end of the players' benches, and two more blower heaters behind each bench, to help keep us warm when we weren't in the game. All in all we were a lot better off than the people in the stands. I'm not sure I would have sat in that ball park for three hours that Sunday afternoon unless they were willing to pay me more money than I got for playing. The wind was pure frostbite. It was about thirty-six or thirty-seven degrees on Saturday, but I thought it was a pretty nice day because the wind wasn't bad. Sunday was something else again.

After the workout we went back to the hotel. There wasn't much to do. We had permission to go out if we wanted to. But the club had a private dining room and lounge set up for our convenience in the Town Room, off the hotel lobby, which was open between six and eight o'clock and where you could order whatever you wanted. All you had to do was sign the check. That was where I went. I wasn't about to go out and face the crowds in downtown Cleveland. There must have been thousands of people in town for the game, at least 8,000 of them from Baltimore alone. I had a very good steak in the Town Room, and then I went back upstairs to the room I was sharing with Jerry Hill. I stayed in for the rest of the night, watching a couple of the bowl games on television.

About half past eight a couple of friends from Baltimore dropped in and sat around and talked for a while and wished me luck. They were the only people who came to see me. I guess the others who might have, like Dorothy's parents, didn't want to bother me. A couple of people called to wish me luck or to thank me for getting them tickets. I got twenty-six tickets altogether, including six for my brother Len. Some of the people who called, of course, I didn't know, but that always happens. There was a young boy who said he was calling for his grandmother and she wanted to know if it was all right to bet on us. I spent a few hours with my play book, going over our offensive plans, and then Jerry and I watched "Gunsmoke" on television for an hour, watched the eleven-o'clock news, and went to sleep.

I was sound asleep when the telephone woke me up at half past twelve. You know how it is when you try to make sense out of what's going on at a time like that. It's bad enough if you know the person you're talking to. But this was a long-distance call from somebody in Carolina, wanting to know how badly we were going to beat the Browns.

"I already bet my house and my farm," the man said. "I need to know, how bad you gonna beat them? Maybe I can get down some more."

It didn't do any good to tell him I wished I knew. He was serious. Then he really made me mad. "I already won two hundred dollars," he said, "just by being able to talk to you." Then he said, "Wait a minute, my wife wants to talk to you."

So he put his wife on and she said, "Hello, boy, you gonna win that game?"

I said, "Good night, lady," and I hung up.

But it took me a long time to get back to sleep. What puzzled me was how the call got through to me in the first place. It's a club rule that they're not supposed to put any calls through to us after eleven o'clock. After eleven o'clock they shut them off, and even your wife can't get you unless she calls one of the officials and gives him a message to have you call her. In fact, in the morning, before breakfast, Jerry called the operator and asked for Fred Miller's room number, and the operator refused to give it to him. She said the club rules didn't allow her to give the number of any player to anybody. "Even another player?" Jerry wanted to know. But she wouldn't give it to him. Yet they let this nut through on my line in the middle of the night.

Early Sunday morning a boy called up and said he had to get my autograph. I said, well, I didn't know if I would have a chance to give it to him before I had to leave for the game. He said, gee, he needed it for his sister, who was going to have a baby. So I said, all right, come on up. And then I had to take half a dozen phone calls from different people about this one boy, had I really given him permission to come up, was it all right, and like that. In the end he got the autograph he wanted, whether it was for his sister or whomever.

Another boy called and asked me, "Mr. Unitas, do you have any spare footballs laying around in your room? I sure would like to have one." It took me five minutes to convince him that I never have any footballs lying around in my room.

After breakfast I went to Mass with Dick Szymanski, Gino Marchetti, and Gino's boy, Ernie, who had come to the game with him. When we got back to the hotel we looked for a place to have a cup of coffee. We saw this coffee shop on the ground floor of the hotel called the Minute Chef, and we went in there and ordered coffee. We hadn't even been served yet when Steve Stonebreaker came barging in the door, looking for us, and said we had to come back and have coffee with him and Shula in the Town Room because the four of us had been having coffee together after Mass every Sunday all season. I was surprised that Steve was so superstitious. It turned out that he had been running all over the hotel looking for Marchetti and me to make sure we had our coffee with him and Shula.

139

We had our pregame meal at half past nine in the Lewis Room, downstairs in the hotel. I had ham and eggs. Some of the fellows had steak, but it was a little too early in the morning for me to have anything that heavy.

At about eleven o'clock I was back in the Lewis Room, where the trainers had set up shop to do the taping. The visitors' dressing room at Cleveland Stadium is so small that our people thought we would be better off if we got taped at the hotel and didn't have to do anything except get dressed when we got to the ball park. Bill Neil, who is with the Crippled Children's Hospital in Baltimore and who was helping out our trainers for the game, taped me. When he was finished I just stayed right there rather than go out and battle the lobby, which was crowded with people standing around looking for football players or anybody else they might recognize. At a quarter after eleven I checked out of my room, signed the bill, made my way outside, signing autographs on the way, and got on the team bus. We took off for the Stadium at eleven-thirty. It was just beginning to snow, but it looked as though it would only be a flurry and wouldn't last. I thought it probably would be as good a day as we had any right to expect at this time of the year in Cleveland. But as we rolled to the stadium the wind began to kick up. By the time we got off the bus it was real windy, and that was the way it stayed for the rest of the day.

In the dressing room it was the way it always is before a game, everybody pretty quiet except for an occasional wise-crack. Whenever we're away from home it's a problem getting all of your stuff together, and that keeps you busy for a while. Getting all your pads fixed and getting dressed keeps you occupied long enough so that you don't have too much time to think about the game and get nervous before it's time to go out on the field.

The boss, Carroll Rosenbloom, came in to wish us luck, the way he always does. He's more nervous than anybody on the ball club. He's more superstitious, too, and I told him about the episode with Stonebreaker and the coffee. He kind of laughed at it, but I could see that he approved, he thought Steve was right. I said I wasn't superstitious, and he said I probably was but just didn't realize it.

Carroll is always needling me, sometimes gently and sometimes a little more sharply. Once, after a game, he said to Cuozzo, "Glad to see you looking good out there, Gary. Maybe, if we're lucky, we can get McHan back for Unitas and a couple of used jockstraps."

"Be my guest," I told him. "I was looking for a job when I got this one. I've always got a bag packed."

I had Bill Neil rub down my right arm and shoulder and elbow. Then the superstition bit came up again. Bobby Boyd wanted to know if I was ready to throw the football some in the dressing room, to warm up. I said I thought it was kind of a small place to be throwing in, and he said we had to throw a little bit, anyway, because we'd done it before every other game and we wouldn't stop now. So we cleared a little area and threw the ball back and forth for about ten minutes until Bobby was satisfied that we had taken care of the tradition.

Our kickers went outside at a quarter past twelve and the rest of us at half past twelve. It was cold out there, and the wind was blowing pretty good. It didn't take me very long to see that it was going to be a bad day for passing. If you threw deep, the wind took the ball and either brought it into the middle of the field or pushed it out of bounds. You really had to put some snap on the ball to get it out through the wind. You had to keep the nose of the ball down so that the wind couldn't get too much of a hold on it. If you threw it with the nose up or with the least little bit of a wiggle on it the wind really grabbed hold of it.

Actually, it didn't bother me so much in the game. It hurt me on only one throw. That was when I made a sideline pass

141

to Jimmy Orr in the third quarter and threw the ball up too high in the air, and the wind took it and just sucked it right down to the ground. That one hurt because it could have been a good play for us if we had been able to complete it. It would have got us a first down, and we might have been in the ball game. But you can sit back and second-guess yourself on things like that all you want to. It doesn't do any good, and it's ridiculous to do it.

We stayed out there for about fifteen or twenty minutes and went through all of our passes. We threw what we call pat and go, Gary on one side and me on the other and our receivers on either side of us. The receivers ran down one side of the field and then down the other, and finally down the middle. It's a good warming-up procedure. Then the whole offensive team ran off pass patterns against the defensive line, trying to simulate game conditions. It was a good, brisk workout, with a lot of enthusiasm, and when we went back inside we all felt pretty good about things. Too good, I guess.

It's easy now to see how much it was like what happened to us in the first game of the season, against Minnesota. Everything seems to be just right. Your workouts are good, your spirit is good, everybody has the willingness to work extra hard, the execution of the plays is clean and snappy. Then you get into the game and everything goes bad on you. That was what had happened to us in the first game. The Vikings just stopped everything we tried to do. They caught our ball carriers behind the line of scrimmage and threw them for loss after loss. They stuck to our receivers like wet snow, and every time I went back to pass there was a hand in front of my face or a foot on my chest. The wicked tackling that our defensive team was so proud of just wasn't there. The blocking was too little and too late. That was how we played against Minnesota in the first game of the season, and that was how we played against Cleveland in the last game of the season.

But sitting in the dressing room before we went out for the kickoff, I thought we were ready for a real fine ball game, with good execution and no mental mistakes. That's always a big part of it. You can excuse a physical mistake because everybody is going to get beat on a play some time or other, but it's the mental mistakes that generally end up killing you. I thought we were sharp, and ready. Then we went out and played a bad football game. We came up with our worst game of the year at the worst possible time we could have done it. We had worked our heads off since July 15 to win the Western Division and get a chance to play for the championship, and then we got out there and played a stinking game. It hurts your pride, and it makes you wonder what it is that happens.

A basic part of our strategy was to play a ball-control game, on the theory that Jimmy Brown can't run for touchdowns against you if he is sitting on the bench while the Cleveland defense plays the game. But it worked the other way around. The Browns won the toss and elected to receive, so they started out with the ball, and it seemed as though they had it most of the day. In fact, they did. They went from their own twenty-one to the forty-nine before they had to kick. We set up shop with the ball for the first time on the twenty-two. Shula wanted me to throw a pop pass on the first play, partly so that he could get a chance to see what kind of a defense they were going to use against our throwing. I went back with the ball and looked for Johnny Mackey, my primary receiver on the play, but Walter Beach had a good hold on him. So I looked for Raymond, my secondary receiver, but he was covered, too, and all I could do was run back through the pocket and go down with the ball. But the officials called Cleveland for defensive holding, so we picked up five yards and an automatic first down.

We were moving the ball all right, and we made another first down. Then Jerry Hill fumbled at the fifty, Dick Modzelewski recovered for the Browns, and although we didn't know it at the time, the pattern of the game was set. Every time we began to get going, we did something bad. We fumbled, or we dropped a strike, or we ran into one of those two crazy interceptions the Browns got on us, both of them on balls that bounced off the receiver's chest and floated up in the air and were picked off like apples off a tree.

With Jimmy Brown doing most of the work, the Browns took the ball to our thirty-four, but we got a break there when Don Shinnick, our right linebacker, intercepted a Frank Ryan pass to Paul Warfield on the ten and brought it back to the twenty-four. Things weren't really going smoothly for us, and I was running with the ball as much as I was throwing it, but we went all the way to the Cleveland nineteen before we were stopped and Shula had to send in Lou Michaels and the field-goal team. The way things were destined to go for us all day, it was inevitable that Bobby Boyd should be unable to set up the ball for the first time in his long career as a holder for field goals and place kicks. The wind took the ball and pulled it away from him, and there was no time to try the kick. When he finally found the handle he picked up the ball and tried to run with it, but the whole Cleveland team fell on him, and that was that.

The first of those two interceptions killed our next good drive. Gary Collins, our chief nemesis, had punted into the end zone, and we took over on our own twenty. We were going along fine and had moved past midfield to the Cleveland forty-two, when we lost the ball on a low pass to Mackey on the thirty. The ball bounced off his body and hung up high in the air, begging to be intercepted. Vince Costello, Cleveland's middle linebacker, obliged.

Another instance of how it just wasn't our day was what happened on the next play. Ryan went back to pass and Gino went right with him. Frank got the ball away, but big Gino

144

blocked it. The ball hung there for a tantalizing second, and Gino almost got his hands on it, but not quite. If he had, it would have been an easy touchdown, because he was all alone, behind Ryan, behind everybody, and the goal line was only twenty yards away. But fate was playing for Cleveland that day. So were Frank Ryan and Gary Collins, and they killed us in the second half.

Charlie Winner and Don McCafferty, the two coaches who sit upstairs during the game and work the telephones to the bench, joined us in the locker room between the halves, and all the coaches tried to cover, in the time we had, the things we had been doing wrong and the things we were going to have to do to win the football game.

We talked about how we had to get our running game going, so it would open things up for the passes, the way it had done all year. It was a sign of how badly off we were that I was our leading runner for the half with fifty-four yards gained rushing. That was very bad for us. The defense always would rather have the quarterback run than pass. We knew we were going to have the ball at the beginning of the second half, because this time the Browns had to kick off to us, and Shula said to call the thirty-four Wham and give the ball to Moore on the first play from scrimmage and try to establish the running game. We had always felt, and we still felt, that our five men up front could blow their defensive men out of there, and we knew we had to go that route or lose. If all they had to worry about was me and my pass receivers, they would bury us. They had to be kept in doubt about what we would do.

I ate a couple of oranges, and I talked a little bit to Raymond Berry and Jimmy Orr, who were sitting on each side of me, and I talked some to Shula and some to McCafferty. Mac always tries to give me some idea of what downs they are blitzing on, and how often. If he sees that they are blitzing a lot on first down, I won't call so many first-down running

145

plays. I might prefer to throw into the blitz, at least for a while, and try to hit certain patterns off it.

The officials came in and gave us the five-minute warning. We put our helmets on and made sure we were all ready to go, and then Shula talked to us. He wasn't real happy. He said we weren't playing up to our capabilities. He told us what we had to do and he said he had faith in our ability to do it. He didn't try to give us a shot of inspiration or anything like that. He sent us back out there, the way he always does, as professionals, to do the job we were getting paid to do.

But we couldn't do it, not that day. I gave the ball to Lenny on our first play, but it just wasn't there. He got about a yard. Then I threw that poor pass to Orr at the sideline, the one the wind took and grounded. I tried another pass on third down, a screen to Jerry Hill, and for a few seconds I thought we were in business, but Jerry couldn't hold it. We had to give up the ball, and it was a bad situation. Tom Gilburg had to kick into the teeth of that wind. He tried to keep the ball low, didn't kick it cleanly, and the Browns had the ball inside our forty. Our defense held them for three downs, but then Lou Groza, the middle-aged businessman's pride and joy, came in and kicked a field goal from the forty-three, and the ice was broken.

We were still nowhere on offense, and the next time the Browns got their hands on the ball they took it sixty-three yards for a touchdown on two plays. Jimmy Brown knocked off forty-six of those yards on a pitch-out that was a thing of beauty. Jimmy is hard enough to stop when he goes straight into the line, but when he has running room, look out. Gang tackling is your only hope. The last seventeen yards were covered in the air, Ryan to Collins, a pass that Frank must have waited a good five seconds to let go.

It was Collins again, all by himself in the end zone, just

two minutes and twenty-two seconds later. That made it 17–0. I thought we still had a chance. We have scored more than twenty points in a quarter often enough to know it can be done. But we knew we had to do it fast. Instead, we just barely got across midfield to the Cleveland forty-eight when Lenny and I messed up a handoff and the Browns recovered the fumble. I think what actually happened was that I pushed the ball right through Lenny's arms. He said he never felt the ball. It was strictly my fault. The ball went right through his arms and out the other side, and the Browns had it. Our side had something to cheer about when the defense stopped big Jimmy three times from the one-yard line, but Groza came in and kicked another field goal, and we were twenty points down. It became twenty-seven when Collins made a fine jumping catch on the ten-yard line and took the ball in spite of everything Jerry Logan could do.

You have to say that Cleveland just wanted the game a little more than we did. They certainly worked for it and fought for it. They beat our pants off. They outplayed us all afternoon.

We fumbled twice.

We had two interceptions.

We bobbled the snapback on the field-goal try.

We dropped one key pass and were ruled out of bounds on another important one. I completed twelve out of twenty passes, which doesn't sound like a bad percentage, but they added up to only eighty-nine yards, the fewest yards gained passing I had had in my nine years in the league.

We weren't good, and we weren't lucky, and it's no wonder we didn't win.

Looking back on it, I would say that Cleveland's linebackers did a great job on us. I didn't feel that their deep secondary was that tight on our receivers. They did pretty much what they had been doing all year, play loosely to defend against the deep pass. But their linebackers took such an intelligent angle on most of their pass coverages that it didn't give me much room in which to throw the ball. If I had a receiver coming to the inside, they always seemed to be in such a position that I could see that, if I threw the ball, they would have a chance to get a hand on it. Like all quarterbacks, I hate interceptions like poison. So when their linebackers dropped back with my receivers, I tried to shake their coverage by running the ball myself. Our linemen were blocking their front four to the outside, and with no linebackers shooting in on me, I had a hole up the middle in which to run. What I wanted was an open receiver, but I didn't find many. Most of the credit, I think, goes to their linebackers and to the coaches who devised the plan those boys carried out so well.

The Browns had the ball on our twenty when the game ended. There were still twenty-six seconds to go when the crowd began to run out on the field. They tore down the goal posts at the far end and were coming after the other set when the referee wisely decided to let the clock run out. I know the referee spoke to Gino and told him what he was going to do, and Gino said, "All right, go ahead, let's get out of here." Frank Ryan came running over and said he still had a couple of plays coming to him, and I guess Gino got a little sore and said something to him. I can imagine. Hollering for another touchdown at that point was rubbing it in. Anyway the referee shot off his gun and we all went into the dressing room.

We were alone for five or ten minutes before Shula let them open the doors for the newspapermen. The first thing we did was say a prayer. Don Shinnick led it, as he always does, saying a few words first and then leaving us to say our own prayers to ourselves. Then Shula talked. He said there wasn't much anybody could say about a game like this. We just got beat, that's all. We got the hell beat out of us. There was no need, he said, to make excuses one way or the other about it. We were outplayed both offensively and defensively. They had a great day and we had a bad day. Why waste words on it?

Naturally, most of the writers headed for the Cleveland dressing room, but there must have been ten or eleven of them in ours, and they asked all the questions you would expect them to ask. I excused myself while I took a shower, but then, while I was getting dressed, I talked to them as long as they wanted me to. They wanted to know if the wind bothered me, and I said no, not especially. After all, the wind was blowing for Frank Ryan, too, and he did all right. It would have been pretty silly for me to have blamed the weather. Dorothy had the right idea when she said, "Hey, Unitas, why didn't you score three touchdowns when you had the wind with you in the first quarter?"

Some writers try to put words in your mouth—after all, it's their job to try to get headline stories—and you have to watch what you say. They would like nothing better than to have you pop off about something. But I agreed with what Neal Petties, one of our rookie ends, said when he walked through the door into the dressing room. "They killed us," he said, and he was right.

Johnny Morrow, the Cleveland center, put his finger on it, too, when he told a reporter, "Don't listen to all those technical discussions. You want to know what happened out there? They made mistakes and we didn't."

Carroll Rosenbloom and Don Kellett came in and shook hands all around and said, "Tough game." Shula had a press conference of his own going on in the middle of the room. "We killed our own drives," he said over and over. "We gave up the ball too often on fumbles and interceptions. We never gave our defense a break." I couldn't argue with that.

I got out of the dressing room as quickly as I could and got on the bus and waited for the last of our players to come out. There weren't many people around. I guess the Cleveland fans had gone off to celebrate, and the Baltimore fans probably had run for airplanes and trains. Either that, or they were drowning their sorrows somewhere. If I were a drinking man, which I'm not, I might have joined them.

Our chartered plane took off at six-fifteen. We had dinner on the airplane, steak or lobster, either one you wanted. It looked good but it didn't taste good—that might have been us rather than the food. After we ate, I played cards with Steve Stonebreaker, Alex Hawkins, Lou Kirouac and Bert Bell, Jr. It didn't surprise me any that I lost again. It was that kind of a day.

The airplane was real quiet. I was tempted once to needle Stonebreaker about all the good it had done us to protect that coffee superstition in the morning, but I decided not to. Nobody felt too much like making jokes. Not even Jim Parker. About all he said was, "My parents knew what they were doing when they went to Troy this morning."

The control tower at Friendship Airport put our plane down a long way from the terminal, and a bus came out to pick up everybody and drive them in to the stadium. The idea was that if we had won there might have been a big crowd there. A few others, besides me, had cars parked at the airport, and a United Airlines man drove us to the parking lot in his own car. Alex Hawkins came with me because his wife, Libby, had stayed overnight on Saturday with Dorothy. We were all invited to a party Rosenbloom was giving at Kellett's restaurant, the Tail of the Fox. There wasn't any victory to celebrate, but Carroll was giving the party anyway.

One thing that happened on the way into the house gave me a turn. I had parked the car in the driveway and was walking with Alex over to the front door, carrying the attaché case that I had used to pack my spare shirt, socks and underwear, when a little boy who couldn't have been any more than eight or nine came running up and asked me what I had in the suitcase.

"Nothing much," I told him, "just some dirty clothes."

"I know what you've got in it," he said.

"You do?" I said. "Well, you tell me, then."

"You've got $5,000 in there," he said. "The man on television said that you lost the game but you were coming home with $5,000 in your suitcase. He said that was pretty good for a day's work."

I wished there was some way I could explain to him that the money I had earned that day wasn't for a day's work at all. It was for a lifetime's work.

When we walked into the house we found out that Dorothy and Libby had had Susie Hill, Jerry's wife, and Jerry Logan's wife, Fanny, in to watch the game with them. Dorothy had baked a ham and made potato salad and deviled eggs for their supper. She had even put three bottles of champagne in the refrigerator for a victory celebration. Then, when the game was over, she said to the girls, "I've never felt so empty in my life. Let's fill ourselves up with champagne. Maybe we'll drink ourselves to sleep and wake up and find out that the game hasn't been played yet." But when they woke up, just before Alex and I came in, they were showing film clips of the game on television and we had still lost, 27–0.

The party at the Tail of the Fox was pretty quiet. It was in a private room, nobody there but the players, coaches, club officials and their wives, and no one felt like making much noise. Carroll gave all of the wives a silver charm bracelet with a disk that had a Colt on one side and on the other side the words *Colts vs. Browns, NFL Championship 1964.* Very neutral. Each of the men got a tie clasp and a set of cuff links engraved the same way. We stayed at the restaurant until about one o'clock in the morning, and then we went back to the

151

house with the Hawkinses and had a couple of beers. They left for their motel sometime around two o'clock, and we went to bed. It had been a long day.

As somebody said to me the next morning, there is an old Lithuanian saying that you can't win them all.

CHAPTER TEN

DOROTHY ALWAYS SPEAKS WELL of the Pro Bowl game because she had such a good time making the trip to Los Angeles with me for the 1962 game. She's a big movie fan, and we went to the 20th Century Fox studios and met Elvis Presley and then went to Disneyland with Flo and Gino Marchetti, and it was the best trip we've had since we were married. But I have different reasons for liking the game, which I played in eight straight years from 1958 (they play the game in January, so that was at the end of the 1957 season) through 1965. It's a wonderful experience for a quarterback to run an offense with personnel like that. The only trouble is that it's hard to decide who to give the ball to. No matter whose signal you call, you know you've got somebody who can go all the way. But that kind of a problem is a pleasure.

They have been playing the game since January 1939, but the first five were different from the game we have now. The idea in the beginning was to have the winner of the championship team play a league All-Star team. In 1950 the present idea, matching the East All-Stars against the West All-Stars, was adopted, and the game has been a success ever since. The winners now get $1,000 apiece and the losers get $800, and everybody has his transportation paid and gets $50 a day for his expenses, over and above the hotel room, which is taken care of.

We usually get out there about a week before the game and practice a couple of hours a day. It isn't as hard as you might think to put together an offense even in the short time we have to get ready. Most of the clubs in the league use pretty much the same kind of formations and plays. The biggest difference, and the thing that causes us the most confusion every year, is the terminology. Different teams have different names for the same things. What we call a slant pass somebody else may call a look-in. What we call a wide flare somebody else may call a circle. Zee, Shake, and Post are different names different teams use for the same pass pattern. It's the same problem a ballplayer has when he is traded from one club to another, except that at the Pro Bowl game we're all in it together and we have only a few days to sort everything out.

Naturally we use fewer plays than we would in one of our own ball club's games. It makes sense to keep them down and reduce the possibilities of making ball-handling mistakes. We generally go with ten or twelve basic running plays and maybe fifteen different pass plays. Then there are situations where you want to do something that has worked for you during the season and you just improvise a play in the huddle—trying to be careful to use basic terminology that everybody will understand. You don't very often try to invent a running play on the spot, but you do make up some pass plays to take advantage of things you can see in the defense. What it is, simply, is that you know the kind of pass you want to throw in this spot, and you tell the receiver what you have in mind and ask him to get out there and catch it.

That's where the terminology problem comes in. The guy will say, Well, what do you want me to do, and I'll say, Well, run a slant. And that's when he's bound to say, What the hell is a slant? And when I get all through explaining it to him, he nods and says, Oh, you mean you want me to run a curl end. But we make out.

Actually, we take care of most of these problems during the week, not only in practice but just sitting around the hotel talking, or eating together. I make it my business to spend a lot of time with the receivers, guys like Pete Retzlaff, Raymond Berry and Ron Kramer, and find out what patterns they like to run best and how they like to have the ball thrown to them. Then I try to accommodate them.

After I find out what kind of patterns my receivers would like to run, I can begin to work out with the coaches the kind of strategy and the kind of blocking they want me to use. Once the game starts it's generally a man-on-man blocking situation, and my principal problem is to see what type of coverage the defensive secondary is using and how I may be able to upset them by careful use of flare control. If I see that they're using a free-safety type of defense in the back, where your weak-side safety man is always free to go and help anywhere he is needed, I go to work to try to control him by sending my close flare back down there straight and deep. Once I have that flare back into the free-safety's territory, he isn't free anymore. He's got to be concerned about our man, he's got to stay with him and take responsibility for him. So now I'm able to work one side or another with whichever receiver I want to use on the play. I can be confident that there will only be one man on him, not two.

The thing that makes the Pro Bowl game so interesting to watch is the same thing that makes it so interesting to play in.

Every man out there is an expert at his position. There isn't a weak sister on the field. They all have a lot of pride in what they can do, and you shouldn't ever get the idea that they just coast out there because it's only an exhibition game. They give and take a lot of lumps. The only thing about the game that is different from the regular-season games is the agreement that there won't be any blitzing of the passer by the linebackers, which is done for the simple reason that there isn't time enough to set up blocking to cope with it. The pass rush is left entirely up to the defense's front four. Other than that, everything goes.

I don't mean to imply that we are worked as hard in practice as our own coaches work us during the season. We practice in the morning and are all through by about half past twelve, which means you have the rest of the day to do what you want —play golf, go swimming, or whatever. Just the same, despite the relaxed atmosphere, you find as the week draws to an end that you're "up" for the game. We all have a great deal of pride in our own division. For years, the teams in the West have thought of their division as not only better but tougher, and we like to prove it.

In the 1965 game, coming just after the Browns had flattened us in the championship and the Cardinals had upset the Packers in the Playoff Bowl game between the second-place teams, we had all the incentive we could ask for. The West's pride was hanging pretty low when we went out to Los Angeles. We wanted to salvage something from the whole end-of-season mess, and we made up our minds during the week that we were going to do it. It might be only an exhibition game, but we didn't intend to play it like one.

For another thing, it was going to be Gino Marchetti's last football game. Both Gino and our middle linebacker, Bill Pellington, had retired after the championship game, but Gino still had this game, his tenth time in the Pro Bowl, to play before he hung up his uniform. Our Baltimore fans had given Gino and Bill a "day" on the Sunday we played our last game of the regular season—each of them got a car, a color television set, a cash purse, and a lot of other things—but this would be Gino's last time wearing number 89. We wanted to make it a good one.

With the front four we had going for us on defense, Gino, Roger Brown of the Lions, Merlin Olsen of the Rams and Willie Davis of the Packers, it wasn't surprising that our offensive team was handed the ball often enough to run up a 34–14 victory. I took my backfield down close enough for an early field goal and a three-point lead in the first quarter, and I ran one long drive in the last quarter that ended with Lenny Moore going over for the touchdown from two yards out. The rest of the time, Fran Tarkenton put on a show for the people. He was at his scrambling best and his passing best, and he richly deserved his selection as the most valuable back in the game, an honor that had come my way three times in other years.

Franny's first offensive series was something to see. He ignored the protection he could have had inside the pocket, just as he does most of the time. He ran around behind the line of scrimmage until he saw Tommy Mason loose, and hit him for forty-five yards. Then he threw for thirty-five more to Terry Barr, who almost made it into the end zone but was tripped and fell on the two. Bill Brown, the big Minnesota fullback who runs a lot like the other Brown from Cleveland, racked up the touchdown. Every time he handled the ball, Fran showed the 60,000 people in the Coliseum and the millions who were watching on television some plain and fancy quarterbacking. Watching him and Tommy Mason and Bill Brown, you knew why a lot of the football writers were saying that the Vikings were the team of the future in the West.

The one unhappy thing about the game was that Frank Ryan got hurt early in the second half when he went back to pass and both Marchetti and Olsen hit him and took him down. Frank came out of it with a shoulder separation, which made everybody feel bad, but especially Gino and Merlin. It was just one of those things. Frank kept trying to twist loose and those two big men weren't about to let him go. Something had to give, and it turned out to be Frank's shoulder.

Don Shula, who coached the West team, was right when he said that our defense was the difference. Our pass rush was something to see. One time it would be Olsen and Marchetti, another time Davis and Marchetti, another time Brown and Marchetti. But it was always Marchetti, bearing down on the poor quarterback like a tough cop putting the arm on a pickpocket. "Both the East's touchdowns," Shula pointed out, "were made off our offense. Mel Renfro got one on an interception off Tarkenton and Bill Brown's fumble gave them the other one. They didn't get anything off Gino and his gang."

Shula was also right when he said that it felt good to win but he would rather have beaten Cleveland on December 27.

I caught a plane for home as soon as I could after the game. From the middle of July to the middle of January, it had been a long season.

CHAPTER ELEVEN

T HEY TELL ME that in the old days baseball or football players who made good money during the season didn't even consider going to work in the off season. They would just go fishing and hunting or whatever it was they liked to do and have themselves a vacation. But things are different now. Times have changed, we all have the government for a partner, and we don't get to keep all of the money we make the way those fellows used to do. The cost of living is higher, too, and it isn't easy to put away much for your old age—or even for your middle age. So most of us try to find something to do in the way of off-season or sideline activities, or both, partly to make extra money and partly to have some kind of a job or business to fall back on when we can't play ball any more.

I was in the bowling business for a few years, part owner of a big company that operated fourteen different bowling houses, but that's a sad story that I will tell you about later on.

Like all athletes whose names get to be fairly well known, I get a chance every now and then to make some side money from endorsements and appearances. Not as much as I might make if I were in New York, which is where the important money is made, but some. Twice they signed up the whole family for television commercials, once cooking hot dogs over a barbecue grill in the back yard, and once, during Easter time, doing a candy commercial. It was for Mary Sue Easter Eggs. It was a singing commercial, and it was probably the worst commercial I've ever seen. I'm shown holding the kids, and all of us, Dorothy and all, are singing "Mary Sue Easter Eggs." Although it was bad, it probably ended up good for the company, because everybody was talking about it. A lot of people even now call me Mary Sue. I can hear them sometimes hollering from the stands, "Get Mary Sue out of there!"

I've done some testimonials for the Baltimore Federal for a couple of years, as have some of our other players. You know— "I put my money in Baltimore Federal," that type of thing. It doesn't pay a great deal of money. In New York, where things are on a different scale, it might be a whole lot different. I've talked to some of the Giant ballplayers and they have told me that if they just go to a banquet there, and it might be only a quick ride on the subway or in a taxicab, they can pick up as much as $300. You go to a banquet in Baltimore, and if it's not free, it's $25. I do a lot of banquets in Baltimore for nothing because it's good for business, and the better the business is for the club the better it is for me.

Frank Scott, the New York agent, gets some jobs for me every once in a while. I've done television commercials for Man Tan and Rapid Shave, and I was a guest host at the Schaefer Center at the World's Fair one time, shaking hands with the people, posing for pictures and signing autographs. I didn't have anything to do with the product. I won't do commercials for either beer or cigarettes. I've turned down two or three cigarette companies for good money, $1,500 a crack for just posing with a cigarette. I don't think it's right to do, because kids look up to athletes and tend to imitate them and I don't want to help any young boy start smoking. I don't smoke myself and never have.

In fact, I spoke at a high-school convention in Washington on the subject of why cigarettes are harmful. They called up and said they would like me to appear along with some other people, including Senator Maurine Neuberger from Oregon, on a panel program about smoking. I said it seemed like a worthwhile cause and I would do it. Then a few weeks later I got a letter from the people running the thing asking me to send them a copy of my fifteen-minute speech. I had to explain that I didn't have the smallest idea how to go about writing a fifteen-minute speech on any topic, even football, and that all I could do was appear on the panel and answer questions and join in the discussion, which is what I did.

I once got into a big hassle when somebody thought I was doing something for beer. That was after the 1959 championship game with the Giants in Baltimore. There was a picture put out by one of the wire services showing me and a couple of the other guys looking happy in the clubhouse. I was holding a bottle of ginger ale, Nehi ginger ale, and it looked just like a beer bottle and the picture was too small for anybody to read what it said on the label. Well, in the following week I must have got a thousand letters from priests, nuns, ministers, Boy Scout leaders, from people all over the country, saying how bad they thought it was that I would pose for my picture holding a bottle of beer in my hand. You're corrupting the youth of the country, they said.

I went down to the Colt office and had Herb Wright, who was the publicity man then, get a big blowup of the picture that plainly showed the Nehi ginger ale label on the bottle, and we sent copies of it to everybody who had written me. But, of course, the correction never catches up with the mistake, and a lot of people still think I had my picture in the paper drinking beer after the championship game.

I often wonder what kind of complaints the guys get who do cigarette commercials all the time. I wouldn't want to have to answer their mail.

One thing I do in the off season that makes very little money but that I enjoy is play with a bunch of the fellows on the Colt basketball team. Fred Schubach, our equipment manager, whose father used to be the equipment manager for the Eagles, runs the team and makes bookings for it. We play at a lot of school and club gyms, against the teachers or the alumni or the club team, to raise money for some benefit. Our squad has Gino Marchetti, Bill Pellington, Jim Parker, Alex Sandusky, Andy Nelson, Bob Boyd, Bill Saul, Jimmy Welch, Don Shinnick, Jackie Burkett and me. We seldom make more than $25 apiece out of the games, but we like to play and the club likes us to get out and meet the fans. Twice we've played against a team from the Philadelphia Eagles at Convention Hall in Philly as a preliminary to a regular NBA game. We got a $300 guarantee for those games—big money, about $30 a man.

The number of games the basketball team plays depends strictly on how we do during the football season. If we have a good football season we're in demand. One year after we won the championship of the NFL we played thirty-three games. In more recent years we've been playing sixteen or eighteen.

What with one thing and another I'm not home very much in the off season. The bookings begin right after the Pro Bowl game, and sometimes it seems as though I'm off somewhere every day in the week. My diary for a typical week in January 1964 showed a trip to Miami to appear at the newest bowling alleys our company had acquired, then two days at home, and then a trip to Pittsburgh for a testimonial dinner to Art Rooney. I went to the dinner with Shula. Kellett and Rosenbloom also flew down for it. The next night I went to Lancaster, Pennsylvania, and then after one day off I had to fly to Petersburg, Virginia. I was supposed to be in Hampton, South Carolina, the next night, so I went from Petersburg to Washington and then down to Hampton, without ever going back home. I got home on Friday and didn't have anything to do until Saturday night when we played a basketball game in York, Pennsylvania.

I make it a rule not to do anything during the football season unless it's something the club has asked me to do. But once the Pro Bowl game is over, and I'm on my own, it's a merry-go-round. Especially if we've had a winning year. When we won the two league championships, I was never home. I was always out somewhere collecting the pieces of silverware that Dorothy has to keep polished down in our playroom.

One business that I don't think I will ever succeed in, although it has been good for a lot of football players, like Kyle Rote and Pat Summerall and Johnny Lujack, for some, is radio and television. I just don't have the gift for it. For a while I used to do a show from the bowling alleys, as part of our attempt to popularize ten-pin bowling, but I didn't know how to keep a running conversation going with the people, and the show wasn't much good. After a while we got a professional, Jack Dawson, who's with WMAR-TV in Baltimore, to do it, and I would just bring on the contestants at the beginning and then congratulate the winners at the end. The show got better right away.

My other big try at show business was during the summer after our 1963 season when Seven Arts, the movie and television company, asked me to fly to Hollywood to make a pilot film for a new television series. The idea was to do a one-hour program, once a week, each one on a different position on a pro football team, using different players from all of the National Football League teams. They picked me to do the quarterback film, and they figured on using that one as a sample to sell the idea to a sponsor. I guess they never got a sponsor, because after that one show was put on the air I never heard anything more about the series. Maybe they should have got a quarterback who was a better actor.

The only way for somebody like me to make any money out of television is by doing guests shots. Like I've been on the Ed Sullivan show and I've been on with Jerry Lewis and with Eddie Fisher. They give you your lines, exactly what you're supposed to say, and they tell you where to stand, and the teleprompter is always there if you forget what you're supposed to say next. It's easy enough to do and the pay is pretty good, anywhere from $500 to $2,000 a show, depending on how big a budget they have, how much they want you to do, and how hot you are at the time.

Two things I wouldn't want to do are have a football program or write a newspaper column of my own during the season. To do it right you would have to be unpleasantly blunt about the men you are playing with and against, and I don't think that would be good for our football team. If I ever got so foolish as to talk or write anything bad about some of the men on the other clubs, it might not be good for me. They all get a chance to take a lot of shots at me, and I don't see any sense in making them mad.

One of these days I will have to look for a connection with a solid firm. Before I got into the bowling thing I had a good off-season job with the Farboil Paint Company, selling for them. Not to retail stores but to industries. I sold quite a bit of paint, for instance, to Bethlehem Steel. Farboil is a big marine-paint outfit, and they gave me a guarantee of so much per week plus a commission on what I sold. It worked out very well for me, and it was something I could do on my own, pretty much in the time I wanted to devote to it. But when the first bowling alley was about ready to open, Kellett suggested that I ought to quit the paint company. I really didn't have to because there was no reason why I couldn't have handled both jobs, but I agreed with Kellett that it didn't seem fair to either the bowling operation or the paint company to let it appear as if I wasn't giving enough of my time to either one. Now I'll have to think about something else.

The worst part about sideline businesses is that they can go bad on you, just as any business can go bad on anybody. It was a big story in Baltimore early in the summer of 1964 when the Brunswick people sued our bowling corporation for $3,000,000 for nonpayment of installments due on our automatic pinsetters. Everybody kidded me about it. The sum involved was so huge that it sounded funny. But not to me. It shook me up pretty good.

The bowling alleys had never done well from the time we opened them. In the beginning I was in it with Carroll Rosenbloom and Don Kellett, my two bosses, and George Banks, who used to be a big owner of Brunswick stock and who was the promoter behind the deal. We opened four brand-new, big, beautiful houses all called Johnny Unitas' Colt Lanes, and even though the Baltimore area has always been strictly duckpin territory, and we were going in with standard-size tenpins, we might have made it if Baltimore County had allowed us to have liquor licenses. But they refused, I guess on the ground that there were too many young people coming into the buildings, and from the time they made that ruling we never had a chance. You can't make money on a bowling alley today unless you can run a bar. I know. I found out the hard way.

I had hoped that we would be able to make it go after a few years. It didn't bother me any that there was no money coming in now. All I was interested in was the chance of building something for the years ahead when I wouldn't be playing football any more. I was also reassured by my understanding with the Brunswick people that there would be no personal liability on my part so far as the corporation partnership was concerned. If the thing collapsed, they had told me right from the beginning, they would simply repossess the pinsetters and that would be that. Of course, that was when they were trying to sell me on the idea of going in on it. They wanted the alleys put up, and they wanted my name on them, and they did everything they could to make me feel safe about it.

The one thing they never would do, though, was send me a formal letter absolving me of any personal liability for the pinsetter debt. I asked them for one repeatedly, but I never got it. I should have realized then that there was more to the deal than met the eye, but I didn't do anything about it.

For the first few years we kept up the Brunswick payments fairly regularly, although it meant we had to let some of our other creditors, smaller ones, wait quite a while for past-due bills. Then we decided to let Brunswick wait while we tried to catch up with what we owed the other people. That made Brunswick unhappy. They got a lot unhappier when Banks swung a deal to have our corporation take over a number of smaller houses in Baltimore, one in Dover, Delaware, and three in Florida, giving us, including the four big ones, a total of fourteen houses. I guess they figured we were just compounding our troubles and making it less likely that they would ever get their money, and maybe they were right. I left things like that pretty much up to Banks. I just tried to help out wherever I could, mostly with forming leagues, making appearances at the alleys, and promotional work like that.

We lost money all three years we were in business. We didn't make a thing. We had hoped that if we could continue for another four years and pay the bills, we would eventually be all right. The only immediate gain we would be getting out of it would be the depreciation deduction we were allowed to take on our tax returns, but at least we would be getting something set up that would be good for the future. And, of course, we always kept hoping that Baltimore County would give in and let us have a liquor license, which would have made all the difference. The bar business would have meant $200,000 a year in revenue to us and would have carried us through the summertime, when bowling is practically nothing. But we didn't get the license, we didn't ever really make the big pins catch on with these duck-pin bowlers, and, like every bowling alley operator in the country, we suffered from the fact that the manufacturers simply oversubscribed themselves. They just put too many alleys in too many places, and killed it. I think they realize it now, but it's too late.

Anyway, it was too late for us. The newspapers carried the story of the $3,000,000 suit on Thursday, July 30, while we were in camp. It upset Dorothy, of course, but I managed to convince her that we would be all right in the end. It upset George Banks, too, but for different reasons. He was mad because the headlines all talked about the suit being against me and Rosenbloom and Kellett. "They didn't even mention my name," he complained to me. I told him if he wanted publicity he would have to go out and make a name for himself.

Alex Sandusky was in partnership with Banks in a house called Revere Lanes, but they got away easy. They were only sued for $49,000. "Just chicken feed," I told Alex. "I'll tell them to put it on my bill."

I remember one day Alex Hawkins—Whitey, we call him—came up to me in the dorm and asked me to lend him three or four bucks for walking-around money until payday. Gary Cuozzo heard him and said, "You're lucky, Whitey. You only need three bucks. He needs three million."

We finally got out of the whole thing, so far as the corporation was concerned, by selling out to a company named Fair Lanes Corporation, owned by some people who had been active in bowling in Baltimore for a long time. They knew all the angles and they had the capital and the organization to put it over. Some day I may work for the Fair Lanes Corporation, but if I do, my ownership interest will be just a token, which is all right with me. I don't want to spend my life in the bowling business. It's too tough.

As far as my contract with the football club is concerned, I have never had any serious trouble. They have always looked at my side of it as well as theirs. I talked to Kellett about my contract for the 1964 season three or four times before camp opened, but I still hadn't signed when I reported to Westminster. The first time we talked about it Kellett asked me how much I wanted and I said $100,000.

He said, "Come on, get serious."

"I am serious," I said.

"Well, you'll have to talk to Rosenbloom," he said.

"Okay," I said, "I was just kidding." So we got down to business.

"What's the matter with last year's contract again?" Kellett asked, and I said no, nothing doing.

He asked me to give him a figure, and I did, and once again he said I would have to talk to Rosenbloom. "Carroll," he said, "will jump out of an airplane when I tell him that."

"You better give him a parachute, then," I said, and we let it go at that for a while.

The next time I saw him Kellett said he had talked it over with Rosenbloom and Carroll thought I was asking for too much. I told him I didn't think so. I admitted that it sounded high, but I didn't think it really was when you considered the whole financial situation of the ball club, television money and all. I didn't see why I shouldn't get some of that money from television. Kellett said, even so, he wished I would sharpen my pencil a little. I told him I wished he would look at it a little more from my side, and we left it at that.

Meanwhile, I kept going to practice every day, working hard, getting ready for the season. He knew I was going to sign, and I knew I was going to sign, but I had made up my mind not to give in too easily. I wanted some concessions from them, and

I could wait right up to the first ball game if I had to. It was a question of how long they could wait.

Actually, they didn't wait long. Kellett called me in a few days later and asked me to sit down with him. "I've been talking with Carroll," he said, "and we'd like you to sign the same contract you signed last year." I started to open my mouth but he motioned me to wait. "Don't say anything until I finish," he said. "There's more to it.

"We're suggesting that we pay you the same base salary you drew last year. If you go to the Pro Bowl again, you'll get a bonus. If you win the Western Division, you'll get another one. If you win the league championship, you'll get another one. And if you sign now, we'll throw in $5,000 more just for signing."

This is when a professional athlete wishes he were an actor or a writer or a musician and had an agent handling his business affairs for him. I thought hard. It seemed to me Rosenbloom was trying to meet me halfway, and I didn't want him to think I was going to be hardheaded just for the sake of being hardheaded.

"Well, I don't know," I said. "Actually, all you're offering me for sure is a $5,000 raise. I'll be glad to take all those extra arrangements, but I'd still like to have the base pay I asked for."

"Then I guess," Kellett said, "we'll have to get Rosenbloom out to the camp here and see if we can't all get together." I said that would be fine with me, I thought it was the best thing to do.

When Rosenbloom showed up, he was ready for me. He's a pretty shrewd businessman, the boss, and he knows when to close a deal. He took the figure they had paid me in 1963 and the figure I had asked for, which was a whole lot higher, and he came pretty close to splitting the difference with me.

"Now," he said, "what I'd like to do is get squared away with you for a few years so we don't have to go through this every summer. Let's make it a three-year contract at this figure. The

169

money will be guaranteed. You get paid for every year of the contract even if you get hurt. We'll take out $100,000 worth of insurance on your life and make your wife the beneficiary. Plus which we'll pay you whatever part of the total you want in deferred compensation, so much a year for as long as it lasts after you retire. That means you're not only getting a substantial raise but you're saving a lot of tax money, too, by taking some of the money later on when your income won't be so high."

I said I would like to think about it a little, and he looked at his watch and said he had to catch a plane at eight-fifteen. I promised I would come to see him before he had to leave.

I have always disliked the idea of signing a contract for more than one year. I believe a ballplayer shouldn't stand still. He should always move ahead as long as he is successful. If you sign a contract for two years or three years, and you have a tremendous season, there isn't anything you can do to capitalize on it. You have traded security for opportunity, and the only way you can get any more money no matter what you do is for the club to give it to you out of the goodness of their hearts. That's not a very businesslike position to be in. On the other hand, so far as my particular problem was concerned, Rosenbloom had hit on a good bargaining point where my taxes were concerned. Like every other athlete whose peak earning years are strictly limited, I have to pay out a heavy percentage of my best pay checks in taxes. This despite the fact that in the years after I retire I may not make anything like the kind of money I do now. As everybody knows, most ballplayers and fighters and other athletes don't make much of anything after they get out of the big money. It seems to me there ought to be some kind of a tax adjustment for people in that kind of a fix. But right now, at least, there isn't, so I was thinking hard about Rosenbloom's offer to pay part of my salary in deferred compensation. I knew very well that that money could look awfully good to me the first few years after I got out of football.

And I didn't expect to be through at the end of three years, so this could be just the start of something very important for me.

A few hours later I sat down with Carroll again and said I was interested in his proposition, if he would improve it just a little bit for me.

He grinned a little and said, "How?"

That's when Rosenbloom really set me back. "All right," he said, shaking hands, "it's a deal. I want that division championship real bad. Win it for me in 1964 and you get an extra $5,000. Do it again in '65 and I'll make it $7,500. Do it again in '66 and it'll be $10,000. How's that?"

Nobody could ask for a better deal. I didn't even mind when he said later, as we were breaking up, that I would understand, of course, that with all of these changes in my favor, they couldn't very well buy that $100,000 insurance policy for me, too. I said I understood and I was satisfied.

A couple of days later Kellett stopped me outside the dorm and asked me what I was doing on Monday.

I said, "Nothing that I know of. Why?"

"I've got a date for you for a physical for that insurance policy for Dorothy," he said.

"You'd better talk to Rosenbloom," I said. "He told me he was calling that off."

But Kellett shook his head. "No," he said. "He called me up yesterday. He changed his mind."

What I liked about the whole negotiation was that there was never any bad feeling. I think, even aside from the specific amounts of money asked for and settled for, that's one of the real problems in the setup we have that forces the athlete to do his own business with his bosses. I think a third party could prevent a lot of bad feeling that comes up sometimes when people can't compromise their differences and end up getting mad at each other. Anyway, there had never been any trouble between

Rosenbloom and Kellett and me, and I was ready to go on and play football as well as I knew how.

I'm still not crazy about the three-year element in the contract, but I recognize that there is a limit to what the game can pay when each club has only seven home games and seven road games, with the gate split 60–40 in the home team's favor. The four or five preseason games have come to be important to the clubs. They bring in a lot of revenue. But the biggest factor in the player's salary is television.

The two-year contract the National Football League signed with NBC for the 1964 and 1965 seasons called for a total payment to the league of $28,000,000. That means $2,000,000 altogether, or $1,000,000 a year, for each club. When you figure that the club's total expenses for the season can't go much over $750,000, you can see that they are about $250,000 in the black before they count a single dollar from the gate. That's what I was thinking about when I pressed for more money. That's what I'm thinking about when I say quite honestly that I think pro football may have its first $100,000 player some time in the next five years. The money is there—and you know they're not going to take less money for the television rights in the future than they are getting right now.

I would like to be that player.

CHAPTER TWELVE

AN AFTERWORD
by Dorothy Unitas

I was Dorothy Hoelle for nineteen years and I have been Dorothy Unitas for ten years. I'm just beginning to understand the problems that go with being married to a man who is so much in the public eye, so famous and so easily recognized that you can't go anywhere with him or use your name in any kind of transaction without being singled out as someone apart.

It's always a problem when you meet people for the first time. You don't know if they are interested in you for yourself or for your name. I suppose worrying about that can get to be a sort of a complex, but it's always there. In the days before Johnny became famous we only had to worry about whether we would eat next Sunday at his mother's house or at my mother's house. When he was earning his pay laying tile or pile driving, we didn't have any social problems, and although I'm grateful for the country-club living that we have today, I also have to live with the constant uncertainty of whether the people I meet are interested in me because of my husband or because of me.

I suppose part of the reason for my feeling the way I do is

that I married Johnny long before he was important. When we were living in a spare bedroom in my father's house, right after Johnny had graduated from Louisville and while he was working on a construction gang, I used to get up at four or four-thirty in the morning to give him his breakfast and pack his lunch and send him off to work. Then I had to occupy myself all day until he came home at about five-thirty. As far as entertainment was concerned, all we had was a television set my father gave us. But we enjoyed it, and the only thing we had to argue about was which channel we would put on at eight o'clock. Now we are capable of arguing for hours about whether or not I'm crazy to think that it would be fun to spend a three-month vacation on a Southern plantation. Johnny thinks that's a ridiculous notion, but I think you should always shoot for something better than what you have.

Johnny has ambitions of his own, of course. He would like, after he is through playing, to become the coach of a professional team. I've heard him say a few times that he would never want to be a coach, that there is too much pressure attached to the job, but I think that as he gets older—and he was thirty-one during the 1964 season—he feels more strongly all the time that coaching is what he ought to do when he is finished as a player. I think he would make a fine coach, because he has one wonderful quality that not every man has—patience.

Even with our four children, Johnny never shows irritation. In fact, he isn't even impatient with me. After all these years of being married to him I'm even shocked when he says he doesn't feel like watching a television show I may have suggested we should look at. For the most part he will do anything rather than argue or fuss about it, and if I have a problem I want to talk over with him it's as easy for me as it is to talk to my best girl friend. Johnny always has time to listen to me, and sometimes that involves a lot of time.

As far as the attention he attracts in public is concerned, that's not any real bother. It's sort of half and half. It helps you get a table in a restaurant, and then it fixes things so that you can't get around to eating for an hour or so anyway. But I'm really kind of flattered that people take the time out to come over and talk to him and ask him for his autograph the way they do. It's nice that they recognize him. I remember once when we had the kids with us in Florida, we went to a drive-in restaurant for hot dogs and hamburgers and I got pretty well teed off when the waitress didn't recognize Johnny. I remember thinking, "This girl is really a dodo, what's with her? She has some nerve not recognizing my husband."

We don't have a whole lot of company at the house, partly because Johnny is away so much. Our relatives come even more rarely. My mother probably comes the most. Both my parents have been a great help to me, but my mother comes every time we want to go away and still be sure the kids are all right. Every time I've had a baby she has come and taken over. I often think Johnny married me because of my mother.

As far as other people are concerned, John likes small, impromptu parties, but he hates big things. We moved into a new house in Lutherville, Maryland, a couple of years ago, and I was proud of the house and wanted us to meet all the neighbors, so I suggested we have a coffee. Johnny said to go ahead and have one. I said I meant I thought we ought to invite all the neighbors in for coffee and cake, and Johnny said, "Fine, you just tell me what day it's going to be and I'll be sure not to be here."

It isn't that he's anti-people, it's just that when he's home he likes to take it easy and relax. For instance, he never gets tired of having the neighborhood kids come around. That doesn't bother him at all, whether they're looking for autographs or dragging him out to play football in the back yard, which he does all the time, no matter how tired he is. When

I want to have a real party, like at Thanksgiving or Christmas or New Year's Eve, I have to sort of sneak around and invite people on the sly and just surprise him. If it comes on him unawares, it doesn't disturb him. He just doesn't like to think about it in advance. It's bad for him to have all that time to feel sorry for himself.

I shouldn't complain about it, anyway, because all he does is save me a whole lot of work. If I'm having a party I start cleaning out all the drawers in the house. I wax the floors and wash the windows. It's a little ridiculous because I know nobody is going to go through the drawers or try to eat off the floor, but it's just the way I am. I want everything spotless, and of course you just can't live that way. So I'm better off having a spur-of-the-moment thing, and it usually works out better that way with Johnny, too. It's better also for the women who come to the house, because the less I offer them to eat the better they like it. Everybody I know is watching her figure and just wants coffee and a cigarette.

The kids are the best. Every time we have moved and have come to know the neighbors pretty well, they have told us to be sure not to let their kids bother us too much. But the truth is, they don't. We enjoy them. Things are always happening, like kids coming to the door and saying, "Mrs. Unitas"—which makes me feel like an old lady right there—"can we have Johnny's autograph?" (I notice they never call him *Mr.* Unitas.) I say, "Come on in a minute," but they never want to come in, no matter how much I insist that it's all right. I generally tell them that I don't have any autographs on loose pieces of paper, but that if they want I will give them each an autographed picture and then they can come back later and Johnny will put their own names on the pictures for them and make it more personal. The kids are always thrilled, but then I end up feeling that I've been pushing Johnny's picture on them as if I were his agent or something.

I do have a sense of pride about him, of course, but Johnny never acts as though he's any different from anybody else, and I would hate to think that I had taken it upon myself to do it. You know, sometimes people say, Oh, you're Mrs. Unitas, and it's as if I should come on as somebody really glamorous, which I'm not. I mean, I try hard to be, but I know better.

It takes as much time to get used to being a football wife as it does to be a football player. At least I think it does. When Johnny was a rookie with the Colts, I was so dumb, and so thoughtless of his feelings, that I didn't think I had to bother to go to the games, because all he was doing was sitting on the bench while George Shaw played. I was a real goof, and I know it must have hurt John that I didn't think it was important enough to go. I should have realized that after what had happened to him, being cut from the Steelers the way he was, he would know better than a lot of players might how much it meant to sit on the bench with the Colts and just belong to the team.

There is an enormous difference between college and pro football. I don't think most people realize the studying and the dedication that the players put into pro ball. They think all you have to be is big, that you don't have to have intelligence. Well, all I can say is that Johnny started working on his play book for the 1964 season in April, three months before he had to report to training camp. All through camp, and all during the season, he sat down and studied the book every night from seven o'clock on. The only thing he interrupted it for was to watch the game movies, either last week's game or some movies of next Sunday's opponent. The kids are always after Johnny to click the machine and make it go backward, which they love. And then I get in there with them, in the den, and the older kids, Janice and Johnny, and I start asking John why that one is doing that and why the other one is doing the other thing. I'm sure John must wish we would all go away and leave him alone, but he sits there patiently and answers all our dumb questions. He insists that it helps him because we pick out different things for him to concentrate on, but I know he's just humoring us. He probably figures, where else can he get coffee and dessert while he watches football movies?

After the kids go to bed, at eight-thirty or a quarter to nine, John goes back to the play book and I usually go upstairs and play records or read. I try not to disturb him, and I try especially hard to get to the telephone as quickly as I can when it rings. Actually, people are very considerate, and we get very few calls during the football season.

We don't go out much during the season. John has Monday off (that's his day to play golf), and sometimes we'll go to a movie after dinner that night, but I'm always doubtful that he really wants to go. He will ask me if I want to go out to a show and we'll get into one of those old-married-people song and dances where I say, You don't really want to go, do you, and he says, If I didn't want to I wouldn't have asked you, and then we go—which is very considerate of him. Otherwise, the only thing we do is to go out to dinner on Sunday night when the team plays at home. We probably would have been going out less if Johnny had caught on with the Steelers, because if we were living in Pittsburgh we would have both our families there, whereas in Baltimore we have made a lot of friends with team families and neighbors—and also have come up with a monthly telephone bill to Pittsburgh that looks like the national debt.

I'm glad that I always encouraged Johnny to try pro football. I firmly believe that if I hadn't, every time he would look at me he would think, Gee, if I hadn't married her, I could have been playing pro football. Which, of course, he had always talked about, and which had always made me wonder why in the world he wanted to play football with those old men. They did look old to me. I think that's easy to under-

178

stand. To a kid of fifteen, pro football players are just a bunch of sloppy old men. But when you get a little older, and get in the game yourself, they are all different personalities, and, in fact, are fantastic people.

Of course, as far as the wives are concerned, we each think our own husband is the greatest, which is understandable, and which is why, I think, I have always tried to sit more or less by myself at the games. I've been thought by some of the wives to be a little stand-offish, but I like to be by myself because when I'm at a ball game I scream. I can't help it. To me, Johnny never throws a bad pass, never underthrows or overthrows his receiver. As far as I'm concerned it's the receiver's fault, or somebody didn't block. Feeling that way, I can yell and holler all I want if I'm sitting alone, but it's not so easy if I'm in a group of wives.

For a long time they used to put all of us in one of two sections, either in Section 9, Row 28, which is where I was, or down in the end zone under cover, where one group of wives liked to sit. I always thought the management was very considerate of us. If any of us were pregnant, they would give us a pass to go up on the elevator—and, believe me, it's pretty far up from the street level to the top of the stadium. There wasn't, of course, much the management could do to protect us against the noisier fans. If you sit in one section week after week, they get to know you, and while it's nice as long as your husband is going well, it can be pretty unpleasant when he starts to go bad.

I remember how I used to get when Johnny first had the bowling alleys and some of the people sitting near me used to holler that he was getting too rich, that he wasn't hungry any more. That's a term I hate, "hungry." But I shouldn't have bothered listening to what they said. That's a mistake. Mary Sandusky, who has always sat next to me, never says or does anything to indicate that she even hears them when they say things like that. When she sees that I'm beginning to get mad, she'll tap me on the shoulder as if to say, Dorothy, simmer down.

Well, anyway, when they put on two new sections in the stadium, about the only wives I know of that they moved out of the old section were Mary and me. It isn't really that I feel I was run out of Section 9, Row 28, but, well, sometimes I wonder. Anyway, when we moved, I tried to be a lady. I decided that, in our ninth season, instead of being a tiger I ought to be a lamb. I'll probably get sheared in the process.

You never know what you're going to get into when you start to talk up. Once, about a year ago, I went to a game with the Redskins in Washington and I got mad when the people sitting near me kept hollering: "We want Cuozzo! We want Cuozzo!"

It just irritated me, that's all, and finally I said to them, "Go on, you don't know a good quarterback when you see one. They ought to put Cuozzo in there for you and lose the game."

It sounded pretty good when I said it, but not so good when I found out that all the people who were doing the yelling were related to Cuozzo and were very nice people besides.

Gary himself is great. I met him at a party a year or so ago for the first time and I thought he was wonderful. He's very adult, for such a young boy, and it doesn't make me a bit mad that he always says he is learning a lot from Johnny. I also like Norm Snead of the Eagles. I think he's beautiful. To me, Norm Snead is a celebrity. But I don't pretend to know anything about the game, I really don't. No wonder Johnny thinks I ought to tend to my cooking and cleaning and let it go at that.

But I do worry about him, even though I try to hide it. Once, I remember, he was hit pretty hard on a blitz and he came off the field limping noticeably. A player's wife sitting near me turned around and said, "Hey, is Johnny hurt or something?"

And I couldn't help saying, sarcastically, "No, he always walks like a farmer."

Then there was the time he had his lung punctured against Green Bay, back in 1958. At first, after the game, they said that he wouldn't be able to play football any more. Well, I sat up with him all night after they sent him home from the hospital with his ribs all taped up, and for a while I wasn't so sure he would even live, much less play any more football. I had to go out to get a prescription filled for him, something that the doctor said would help him breathe more easily, and it turned out to be not so easy. Most of the drugstores in Baltimore are closed on Sunday night. But I finally found one open, a good twenty-minute drive from the house, and when he gave me the package I said to the man, "Will that help my husband breathe better?"

The poor man just looked at me. I guess I figured that everybody in the world was worrying about Johnny Unitas' health, and this man probably never had heard of him. I went outside, and it was raining, and I couldn't remember for a second where I had parked the car, and there I was standing in the rain with the water pouring down my face and my neck, and I was crying. I was a real mess.

Then, when I got back to the house and gave Johnny the medicine, he was watching the Ed Sullivan show on television, and there was a comedian on who struck me as really funny, and I couldn't help laughing. And from then on I was all right. So was he.

I don't know what I would have done if he hadn't been. We got married so young that it's hard to remember what it was like before. Johnny was still in his senior year in college when we got married, and I had a job in Pittsburgh. The wedding was on Saturday and we left right after it for a trip to Niagara

Falls in an old beat-up jalopy Johnny had. We didn't get to the Falls until Sunday morning, and we were back home Monday night. I got homesick for my mother. Honest to God. I cried and cried and cried. Once, after he had agreed to take me home and we were actually on the way, we stopped at a roadside restaurant for hamburgers, and when we sat down at the counter I started crying again. Johnny had to ask the man to put our hamburgers in a bag so we could eat them in the car. Some honeymoon.

We lived with my parents for eight or nine months after Johnny's graduation, and then, after the Steelers cut him and he got a construction job as monkey man on a pile-driving rig, we had an apartment that we paid $75 a month for. I think at first the only furniture we had besides a bed was a kitchen set, which we still have. If you took a bath on Sunday, the water might run out of the tub by Tuesday. When you got up at night to give the baby—it was Janice Ann—a bottle, the waterbugs were so big that the only thing we could do was pick up one of Johnny's heavy work shoes and squash them.

We were happy, though. We're happy now, too, but I think at that time I felt more as if I was contributing something. Don't ask me what, because I was always pregnant, but I guess I felt that we were doing everything together. We were together more than we are now, when Johnny has so many obligations and so many places he has to go. In those days it was a big night out when we went to visit one of our relatives. For a real celebration, we would get my mother to come over and baby-sit while we went to the movies. But they were happy times.

When Johnny was playing with the Bloomfield Rams and was getting paid that famous $6 a game, he used to turn over the money to me on Sunday night or Monday morning and I would get my mother to come over and I would go into town and spend from ten o'clock in the morning until four in the afternoon shopping. I would come home with a brand-new dress and a toy for the baby, yet. Don't ask me how I did it. Now I can't even go to the beauty shop for $6. Which is probably why Johnny handles all the money and just gives me what he thinks I need to run the house. The checking account is in his name, thank God. If anything ever happened to him I would need a business manager and a legal adviser to help me.

Actually, we don't live extravagantly, partly because we have always known that some day when John is through playing we may have to adjust to an entirely different kind of income. We have a beautiful home, for which I'm grateful to Johnny, and we have money set aside for the children's education, and we try to live well within our means. I only have two charge accounts, one in a department store and one in a dress shop, and I try hard not to overspend. I have a girl who comes in two days a week to help me with the laundry and the cleaning, but I could live without her. I suppose my mother and father spoiled me in some respects, and John has helped the cause along some, but one thing I was brought up to do was to work hard, and goodness knows John was, so I don't worry about the future. It would be nice if he stays in football, but if he doesn't, we'll manage. And if he does, I'm going to be the most inconspicuous coach's wife there ever was. I'm not going to know anything. I keep thanking my lucky stars that despite the way people make so much of him these days —especially when the ball club is winning—Johnny himself is no different than he was when I first saw him in the study hall at St. Justin's. He sat next to a boy we all called Twinkletoes because he was such a good dancer, and once when I bought some raffle tickets from Twinkletoes he made me write down my telephone number on the stubs and Johnny copied it down. But he never had the nerve to call me, so we didn't really meet and talk until we were on the basketball bus one day going to a game.

I was standing in the aisle with a few of my girl friends and we went through a big thing with the boys about whether they should give us their seats or not, and we kept saying they needed to sit down because they had to play, but finally we took the seats and that started Johnny talking to me. He told me to save him a seat next to me on the way home. During the game I caught him looking at me a few times, and of course the reason I caught him at it was that I was looking at him all the time.

When we got to my house the porch was occupied. My sister and her boy friend had got there first. So Johnny and I kept walking around in the snow, holding hands and talking, and by the time we finally walked up to the front door the snow was piled up six inches high on our bare heads.

The next day Johnny called up while I was vacuuming the dining-room rug. I never even heard the telephone ring, but my mother answered it and called me and said, "It's a boy who says his name is John Unitas." I ran over to the phone so fast I almost tripped over my own feet. He asked me if I wanted to go to the movies with him, and of course I said yes, and that was our first date.

It was interesting that my mother liked him right away. She always says we got along so well because I'm such a good talker and he's such a good listener. But she always thought a lot of him.

I remember once, when I was first talking real serious to her about him, I said, "Don't you think he's real handsome?"

And my mother looked at me and said, "No, I don't think he's handsome, Dorothy, but I think if you marry him you'll never have to worry about where your next meal is coming from."

Having a date with John was a good preparation for being

married to him. He would come over to the house, I would talk and he would say yes or something like that once in a while to show he was listening, and I would fall asleep on the couch while he watched television. After an hour or so I would get up and make him a sandwich, and then he would go home. But we liked to be together, and except for the fact that I liked to dance and he didn't, and still doesn't, we've always found it very easy to relax with each other.

I did get mad at him once, way back in those days. I guess I thought he wasn't paying enough attention to me or something—you know, that he was taking me for granted. I was a little bit jealous, too, of this other girl who had eyes for him, and maybe I wanted to test him.

Anyway, I wrote him a letter and told him it would be better if we broke off and that I didn't want to see him any more. I couldn't resist telling him to be sure to take her out right away.

So he did, but he told me later that he had to wait an hour and a half for her to get ready, and that she was very dull and it hadn't been worth it. I should be honest and say I was the one who did the making up. I was miserable, and when he said he was, too, I figured, well, Dorothy, that's enough of this nonsense.

We've been married more than ten years now, and a lot has happened to us, but Johnny hasn't changed a bit. When somebody writes him a fan letter, he answers it. He would even send out all the handkerchiefs and things they ask for if I didn't put a stop to it. He takes care of the kids for me when I have to go out, and he still helps me clear the table after dinner.

I always remember how surprised John Steadman, the sportswriter, was the morning of the championship game with the Giants in 1959. It was our home game, and that was before Weeb Ewbank made the ballplayers check in at a hotel Satur-

185

day night before the game—a practice Don Shula has kept up. I don't think any of the players like it, but the coaches seem to think they get a better night's rest and a quieter morning that way.

Anyway, John Steadman wanted to see how Johnny spent the time before the big game, so he came by the house and drove Johnny to eight-o'clock Mass at Immaculate Conception Church on top of York Road in Towson. When they got back to the house I had breakfast all ready—orange juice, two eggs, sausages, coffeecake and coffee for Johnny—and we talked about the weather while they ate. It was cloudy outside but I had been listening to the radio and the weather man was saying it would be clear.

"Rain before seven, clear before eleven," I said, and Johnny just grunted.

"Yeah," he said. "All I hope is I don't have to throw a wet football all afternoon."

My mother was staying with us for the game, so she and I took Janice and Johnny to church at ten o'clock, leaving the two Johns to look after Bobby, who was about a year and a half old, and the new baby, Chris, who was only about ten days old. While we were gone, Johnny changed Chris's diaper, and did it very well, too. He also cleared the breakfast dishes, and when I got back, the kitchen was all picked up.

When I'm tensed up about something, I like to clean up a storm. I'm liable to take down all the curtains and wash and iron them and put them back up. It's my way of working off steam. But, with Johnny, doing these things was just his way of being nice to me, giving me a hand while he had a little time to do it. About the only way he ever used to show that he was nervous on a Sunday morning before a game was when he would retire to the bathroom a couple of times with the Sunday paper. When he did that a couple of times, I knew he was nervous. But that happened very seldom.

I really think Don Shula is missing a bet not letting the boys stay home Saturday night the way they used to. Johnny claims I have never learned how to fry bacon or sausage. He says it's always too greasy when I do it, and as a result, the eggs are greasy, and nothing annoys him more the morning of a game than greasy bacon and eggs. But he would never say anything about it. He would just get up and take a napkin or a paper towel and very gently blot them.

It never fails. I could cook eggs for 200 people and the yolk would never break on one of them, but the day of a football game I would break the yolks on Johnny's eggs every time, and he hates that almost as much as he hates greasy eggs. But I always figured that it was because I had filled him up with that greasy bacon and those broken eggs that he was able to keep his feet on the ground and throw the ball well. If Shula would let him stay home and have breakfast with me, he would keep his feet on the ground all right.

Every once in a while, when the kids are giving me a bad time, I think to myself that there must be an easier way of making a living than getting married and raising children, but I'm always ashamed of myself for even thinking it. Being Mrs. John Unitas is the only thing I ever wanted to be. I consider myself blessed. Not just because Johnny is so successful, but because he is the kind of man he is. He's the kind of man to whom you can say, after he has had a bad game, "It looked good from where I was sitting," and then say, after he has had a good game, "You're not so hot, Unitas. I thought you looked a little sloppy out there today. You better watch out or Cuozzo will be taking over." And he will understand what you are trying to do. He doesn't need me to tell him how great he is when he has had a good day out there. Everybody is telling him. The times I can help are the bad times.

He had one of those bad times a few years ago, and I'll never forget it. Little Johnny was only six, I remember, and we were sitting near a Colt fan who spent all afternoon getting on John. "Unitas, you're a bum!" he kept hollering. "You're all washed up. Why don't you get out of there and let somebody take over who can do the job?" He said worse things than that, too. I didn't mind for myself but I minded for little Johnny. He looked as though he was about to cry.

And then, when the Colts blew another chance late in the game, and Johnny's passes hadn't connected, this lovely man tapped our six-year-old boy on the shoulder and said, "Well, little Unitas, I hope you're satisfied. That's your father out there. He ought to be ashamed of himself."

I was so mad I knew if I said anything to him at all I would explode, so I just shut my mouth and took little Johnny's hand and went downstairs to wait for John outside the locker room. We stand down there in a long, narrow hallway, all the Colt wives and friends of the players, and I was busy talking while we were waiting, so I didn't pay much attention to my son. But when big John came out, and I kissed him, I looked around for little John and saw that he was standing all by himself over in the corner, not even looking at his father. It was as plain as if he wore a sign that he was ashamed, just as that loudmouth upstairs had tried to make him be.

I grabbed him and stood him up in front of me over in that corner and I told him I didn't ever want him to be ashamed of his father again, not ever, that nobody can win every game and that what that man had said didn't mean a thing. "Your father," I told him, and I never meant anything more in my life, "is the best football player in the world."

There. John would never say it, but I will.

188